T0157076

I Love You!

from the Heart of the Father

GOD REALLY DOES LOVE YOU, YES, "YOU," WHOEVER YOU ARE!

MATTHEW DEBORD

WestBow
PRESS
A DIVISION OF THOMAS NELSON

Copyright © 2010 Matthew DeBord

All rights reserved. No part of this book may be used or reproduced by any means, graphic, electronic, or mechanical, including photocopying, recording, taping or by any information storage retrieval system without the written permission of the publisher except in the case of brief quotations embodied in critical articles and reviews.

WestBow Press books may be ordered through booksellers or by contacting:

WestBow Press
A Division of Thomas Nelson
1663 Liberty Drive
Bloomington, IN 47403
www.westbowpress.com
1-(866) 928-1240

Because of the dynamic nature of the Internet, any Web addresses or links contained in this book may have changed since publication and may no longer be valid. The views expressed in this work are solely those of the author and do not necessarily reflect the views of the publisher, and the publisher hereby disclaims any responsibility for them.

Any people depicted in stock imagery provided by Thinkstock are models, and such images are being used for illustrative purposes only.

Certain stock imagery © Thinkstock.

ISBN: 978-1-4497-0848-1 (sc)
ISBN: 978-1-4497-0847-4 (dj)
ISBN: 978-1-4497-0886-3 (e)

Library of Congress Control Number: 2010940642

Printed in the United States of America

WestBow Press rev. date: 12/28/2010

TABLE OF CONTENTS

INTRODUCTION

"I love you!" Are there any more precious words in all of language? Certainly, in the midst of the most treasured vocabulary, these three are always included. Yet, what do they mean? And do people speaking them really speak the truth? Also, do they speak those words defining them the same way I do?

There are so many questions about love, yet we must press on and pursue its essence, for life without love is no life at all. So, please, come with me as we probe into the heart of God, the One whose essence *is* love (1 John 4:8), and let us find the fullness of life in Him.

There are, as we all know, many different types of love we experience. There is the love of friendship, the love of family, sexual love, and emotional love. There is love for mankind, love for nature, and love for all that satisfies the senses ("I love music, ice cream, football, shopping, etc."). There is conditional love and unconditional love.

My purpose in this book is not to outline the different kinds of love, but to pursue the question, "Does God love me?" whoever "me" is. Very specifically, does He love me with that kind of love called "God's love" or "agape love" or "unconditional love"?

Let me very carefully say that beyond any shadow of a doubt, according to the Word of God (the Holy Bible), God loves you (whoever *you* are), and He does so with a very wonderful, powerful, and perfect love. As mentioned earlier, God *is* love! The very essence of His being is love, and that is indeed very specifically "agape" love. This faithful, sacrificial love is unconditional, not even conditioned by what some call "predestination." God's love is there for the receiving and enjoying. You simply must accept it, trust it, yield to it (a multitude of response phrases could be used here), or you can choose to reject it.

Remember, the question is not just, "Does God love?", but the point is, "God *is* love!" No matter who you are or what you have done, God is love.

It has broken my heart to see so many people struggle with their relationship with God, all along wondering, "Does He really love *me*?" There is a very popular belief that everything that happens is a direct word of order from God's throne, that all of life is "predestined" by God, and that we are simply pawns that are moved in whatever direction God has decided (forced) for us. This belief claims that we become and experience just that which He has determined for us to become and experience, and we have no choice in the matters of life. This concept of God's predetermining every detail of life's circumstances includes our eternal destiny.

When I speak of predestination in this light, let me be very careful to define exactly what I mean. Some people believe, and therefore, very emphatically say that God, before the beginning of time, decided (by some arbitrary or "sovereign" means) who would go to heaven and who would go to hell (and this decision had nothing to do with God's foreknowledge of who would respond to Him in faith and trust).

In other words, if you define predestination in some other way, you must then adjust your vocabulary for the process of reading this book. For if every time you come across the word *predestination* in this book, you think of your definition and not this one, then you will miss the entire essence of what I'm trying to say, and our discussion will be reduced to semantics and not theology. So, again, please understand that when I speak of predestination, I am speaking of the following:

> PREDESTINATION: Before the beginning of time, God decided, by some arbitrary or "sovereign" means, who would go to heaven, and who would go to hell, and that decision had nothing to do with any response of faith on man's part, nor God's foreknowledge of such a response.

Whereas I recognize that the Calvinist doctrine includes many various avenues of thought, I will often use the term *Calvinism* to speak of this concept of predestination.

The Westminster Confession of Faith says (chapter 3, parts 2 and 3), "Although God knows whatsoever may or can come to pass upon all supposed conditions, yet hath He not decreed anything because He foresaw it as future, or as that which would come to pass upon such conditions. By the decree of God, for the manifestation of His glory, some men and angels are predestined unto everlasting life; and others foreordained to everlasting death." Part five of chapter three states, "Those of mankind that are predestined unto life, God, before the foundation of the world... hath chosen, in Christ, unto everlasting glory... without any foresight of faith..." Part seven of chapter three says, "The rest of mankind God was pleased... to ordain them to dishonour and wrath for their sin, to the praise of His glorious justice..."

This confession is very popular among those supporting the Calvinist doctrine. Yet *never* does the Bible *say* what I just quoted from it! Whereas the Scriptures do use forms of the word *predestination*, they do not develop the theology as it is defined by sources like the one above. Since the Bible speaks of the foreknowledge of God (Romans 8:29), I see no reason to deny its impact in the working of God.

Those things He has "predestined" for us (becoming conformed to the image of Christ, being adopted as shown in Ephesians 1:5, etc.) are wonderful blessings that God predetermined for those He "foreknew" would place their faith in Him.

I do not deny that it all begins with God, is enabled by God, and is completed by God. But I simply report that God, who indeed is sovereign, expresses in His own Word that He has given us a choice. We can either receive His grace by faith and trust, or we can choose to reject it. Now the Bible declares (actually *says*) this truth from one end to the other!

Please do not misinterpret my motive in writing this book. I have no desire to spend this time and effort in verbalizing all this just to prove my belief correct and someone else's incorrect. My motive comes first of all from the Word, "Man shall not live by bread alone, but by every word that proceedeth out of the mouth of God" (Matthew 4:4 – KJV). We must live by the Word and the Word alone!

We must not submit to man's wisdom or logic, nor shall we accept his crafted systems or structures of theology. As you read through the host of Scriptures found in this work, listen to exactly what the Bible *says*, and *how* it says such. Let the Holy Spirit share with you His own character and activity. Disregard, if you must, what I say, but be sure to listen to the very words of God.

Secondly, my motive comes from having been loved by God, developing a love for others as a result, and longing to see them find the joy, comfort, peace, and fullness that comes from knowing the love of God.

Upon asking a friend one day, "Do you know for certain that you have eternal life?", the response was, "I hope so! I hope God chose me!" Having been indoctrinated with the concepts of Calvinism, this dear friend lived without peace or security, and without knowing God's love. How saddening this was when I heard it! This friend was living with no hope for assurance, inner peace, or joy.

Other than those struggling with the limitations placed upon them by Calvinism, there are a host of people with low self-esteems, difficult pasts, troubled presents, and unsure futures, who wonder if God loves them. I hope the expression of this work will assure them that He does. Even though the focal point of discussion will often speak directly against the teaching of predestination in Calvinism as defined above, I pray that the joy in the host of Scriptures referenced here will encourage you to run to Christ, who loves you beyond your imagination.

Please notice this is not the work or compilation of other authors. In other words, it is not just another restructuring of man's thoughts. It is a simple sharing of God's Word. While writing this book, there were many times I thought, "I just need to sit down and read the Bible with them." With that obviously not being possible, please accept this sketch of the scriptural truth: *God really does love you, yes, you, whoever you are!*

The Westminster Confession of Faith states (chapter 1, part 9), "The infallible rule of interpretation of Scripture is the Scripture itself: and therefore, when there is a question about the true and full sense of any Scripture (which is not manifold, but one), it must be searched and known by other places that speak more clearly." I cannot agree more. We all must be very diligent to do just that.

We must know that God's Word will not contradict itself, and that no other source can help us interpret a passage better than other places in the Bible that speak to similar matters. That is why I have built this book on truth found in God's Word, and not by writing a page by page rebuttal of someone else's book, a compiling of other authors' thoughts, or a confession of faith. I have simply utilized Scripture after Scripture after Scripture!

The only outside source used in this work is *The Westminster Confession of Faith* of 1646. Basically, it was employed to enlighten those not familiar with the strong assertions of the doctrine of predestination. Again, time was not allotted to do a page for page refutation of the volumes written on Calvinism (nor was that my desire). May the simple expression of God's Word bring the truth to light!

You will notice that I have deliberately taken the time and space to type out a multitude of verses, knowing that many people would not take the time to look up all the references themselves. But if you are truly seeking God's face in this matter, *you must take the time to read all the passages which speak on these matters* (and do that within their context). This will greatly enhance your concept of the truth of God's Word. Therefore, in this and any other study, open your Bible and keep it open, so that you can carefully examine the Scriptures as you go along. Be "more noble," as those in Berea (Acts 17:11).

You will notice that as I write I use a lot of parenthetical phrases. When I place words in parentheses, I am simply trying to clarify the meaning of the previous words and phrases. You will also notice that I will put words within quotation marks or in italics. This is obviously for emphasis, again trying to clarify the focus of the thought. Often, words in quotes refer back to Scripture references I have just mentioned.

When I italicize some of the words of typed out Scripture passages, please realize that this has been done to reveal the point of focus in the discussion. It is in no way an attempt to alter the Word of God.

The Scriptures I have inserted are drawn from the following translations:
NASB - New American Standard Bible (not the *updated* version)
KJV   - King James Version
NKJV - New King James Version
RSV   - Revised Standard Version
ESV   - English Standard Version
HCSB - Holman Christian Standard Bible

"For this reason, I bow my knees before the Father,... that you... may... know the love of Christ which surpasses knowledge, that you may be filled up to all the fullness of God" (Ephesians 3:14–21 – NASB).

CHAPTER 1

I Love You, Because That Is Who I Am!

"God is love" (1 John 4:8, 16 – KJV).

If you are a generous person, the people around you will be affected by your generosity, not because *they* did anything, but because of who you are. If you are a talkative person, the people around you will be affected by your outgoing nature, not because of their own personalities, but because you are simply being *you*. Have you ever heard someone say, "I'm sorry! That's just who I am!"? Well, the truth is, God is love, and He loves you, because that's who He is!

God has always been love. Many people have the misconception that God is hard and judgmental in the Old Testament, but Jesus is loving and kind in the New Testament. Nothing could be further from the truth. "Jesus Christ is the same yesterday and today and forever" (Hebrews 13:8 – RSV). The Old Testament Scriptures are about Jesus (John 5:39). Exodus 34:6–7, a passage early in the process of God's revealing Himself to the Israelites, expresses the proclamation from God Himself about His own love. The Old

1

Testament Scriptures are filled with descriptions of God's love and compassion. The Book of Hosea expresses God's love in a most unique way. God's love in the Old Testament is exactly the same love we find in Jesus Christ in the New Testament. We simply are seeing the full revelation of that love in the life and Person of Christ. And, indeed, it is the *same* love, for He is the same God (John 1:1–18 and 10:27–31).

Have you ever come to a point of despair in your life where it seemed that everything was falling apart and your sense of well-being and usefulness was fleeting? One day when I felt I was at the "end of my rope," I was sitting on the floor of my bedroom in great distress and depression. I was very unhappy with my circumstances in life, and I was very discouraged by the way I had handled some of those difficult moments. In my emotional state, I cried out, "God, do you even love me?" Now, certainly I knew in my heart and mind that God loved me and that life was not "over," but my emotions could not help but long for the assurance and comfort that God did love me. I also immediately added to my cry, "I guess You don't have any reason to love me, do You?" Now, I said this in reaction to my own sense of worthlessness and sinful behavior. Immediately, from the halls of eternity, descending from the very throne of God, His voice pierced my soul with these most glorious words (not audible), "Matthew, I never had any reason to love you to begin with." I cannot tell you the joy that flooded my soul upon hearing these words. For as humiliating as they may sound to the world, to me they were ever so comforting and assuring. For my Heavenly Father had expressed that His love for me was not conditioned upon my performance, but was always present in its fullness because that's who He is! And because I had placed my faith in that love (*in Him*), indeed nothing "will be able to separate us from the love of God in Christ Jesus our Lord" (Romans 8:35–39 – ESV). God does not love us when we are good and hate us when we are bad. He died for all of us while we were "ungodly," "sinners," and His "enemies" (Romans 5:6–10). Once we respond to Him in faith and become children of God, He leads us to be good (in paths of righteousness – Psalm 23:3), and He disciplines us when we do wrong (Proverbs 3:11–12).

God's love is truly unconditional, but He does not force Himself upon us. His love is offered as a free gift (Romans 6:23). We must choose to receive it (Joshua 24:15 and Proverbs 1:29). "His own" chose not to receive Him, but those who do receive Him ("believing" in Him, exercising faith) are given the power to become the children of God (be born again, or born "of God" – John 1:10–13).

"In this is love, not that we loved God, but that He loved us and sent His Son to be the propitiation for our sins" (1 John 4:10 – NKJV). God did not send Jesus to us because our love for Him was so great, for we fail miserably in our devotion to Him. God sent His only Son that He might express the fullness of His own character and nature, revealed in the indescribable gift of love in Christ Jesus (2 Corinthians 9:15).

Have you ever heard the expression, "like father, like son"? What does that mean? Well, it means that when you see a young man behaving in a certain way, you recognize in him the character traits of his father. You notice that he has become like his father. The children of God, all throughout Scripture, are commanded to be loving. Why? Well, because that's who the Father is. Notice in Matthew 5:44–45 (NASB) it says, "But I say to you, love your enemies, and pray for those who persecute you." Why in the world would Jesus tell us to do that? "…in order that you may be sons of your Father who is in heaven; for He causes His sun to rise on the evil and the good, and sends rain on the righteous and the unrighteous." Why does He do that? Because that's who He is! He demonstrates His love toward all mankind. Notice how Luke develops this truth about God in Luke 6:27–38. The very reason we are called to treat *all* others in this manner, even our enemies, is because our Father wants us to be like Him, and He *is* this way to *all*. "He Himself is kind to ungrateful and evil men" (Luke 6:35 – NASB).

Remember Jonah? Why did he not want to preach to those in Nineveh? Because he knew that God was "a gracious and compassionate God, slow to anger and abundant in lovingkindness, and one who relents concerning calamity" (Jonah 4:2 – NASB). God Himself says to Jonah, "should I not have compassion on Nineveh, the great city in which there are more than 120,000 persons..." (Jonah 4:11 – NASB). God had compassion on every single person in Nineveh. Why? Because that's who He is!

"But when He saw the multitudes, He was moved with compassion for them..." (Matthew 9:36 – NKJV).

In other words, to be like the Father, we must love others, for God *is* love! How many of these "others" are we to love? Well, how many of them does God love? He loves all! Certainly, we would not think He is kind only to certain "elect" ungrateful and evil men (Luke 6:35). Nor would we presume the Bible is saying that God only had compassion on some of the 120,000 people in Nineveh. When He saw the multitudes, the Scriptures clearly imply that He had compassion on every individual, not just some of them.

So the truth is God loves *all* people! This brings us to our next chapter. This God, who *is* love, shares His love with all people, and that includes you and me!

CHAPTER 2

I LOVE YOU, YES, "YOU" (WHOEVER YOU ARE)!

"For God so loved the world, that he gave his only begotten Son, that *whosoever* believeth in him should not perish, but have everlasting life" (John 3:16 – KJV).

This passage, undoubtedly one of the most (if not the most) popular Scriptures of our day, is challenged constantly. It is challenged by questions like, "Is the word *world* a generic term, or does this verse really include *me*?" Did He really mean to say *whosoever*, or does He really mean just certain people? Does God really love every person, or is this just a general description of His usual disposition? Is Christ's death on the cross a true act of impartial love, or is it simply the legality of a purchase agreement for the sake of some predetermined human beings?

It is amazing how much violence is done to the scriptural text when human reasoning is promoted. Consider the question, "Does any person (do all people) really have a chance to know God and experience eternal life?" According to the source I quoted in the introduction, along with many others who support Calvinism on predestination, the answer would be a definite, *"No!"* Many Calvinists believe that only certain persons can know God, while others have no chance whatsoever!

Rather than relying upon man's logic, let's look to the Scriptures to find God's answer to this question.

The two verses preceding John 3:16 preface this declaration of God's love by giving reference to the Old Testament story of the bronze serpent. Go back and read the story in Numbers 21. Of all the people who had been bitten by those poisonous snakes, how many of them could have looked at the bronze serpent and found healing? God told Moses, "Make a fiery serpent, and set it on a pole; and it shall be that *everyone* who is bitten, when he looks at it, shall live" (Numbers 21:8 – NKJV). That is why when Jesus related this story to the cross, He said, "that *whoever* believes in Him should not perish but have eternal life" (John 3:15 – NKJV). Praise the Lord! Everyone (and that's each one of us) who has been bitten by Satan and has the poison of sin in his spiritual veins, can look upon Jesus in faith ("believing"), and live!

The verse after John 3:16 says, "For God did not send His Son into the world to condemn the world, but that the *world* through Him might be saved" (John 3:17 – NKJV).

Speaking of Jesus, 1 John 2:2 says, "He Himself is the propitiation for our sins, and *not only for ours,* but also for those of *the whole world*" (HCSB). Can this be any clearer? I believe "the whole world" covers it, don't you? The scope of God's plan of redemption is *the whole world!*" Jesus' death is the atoning sacrifice, the payment for sin ("propitiation") for the iniquity of the whole world, *not only for ours!*

Jesus stood up on "the great day of the feast," where multitudes of people were gathered and said, "If *any man* is thirsty, let him come to Me and drink" (John 7:37 – NASB).

Again, Jesus said, "If *anyone* would come after me, let him deny himself and take up his cross and follow me. For whoever would save his life will lose it, but *whoever* loses his life for my sake will find it" (Matthew 16:24–25 – ESV).

These verses, along with a host of others, clearly reveal that God offers His salvation to *anyone, any man, whoever,* and *the whole world.* Calvinists must qualify (actually *change*) the very wording of these verses to bring God's Word in line with their own beliefs.

Imagine at the end of a worship service the preacher says, "If any one wants to see me, I'll be down front following the service." Who is he excluding? None! Every single person within the sound of his voice is being invited and can actually come to see him at the end of the service. This is the very nature of the call of Christ over and over in Scripture. Any person can come to this Christ who "lighteth *every man* that cometh into the world" (John 1:9 – KJV)!

Paul exclaims, "For I am not ashamed of the gospel of Christ, for it is the power of God to salvation for *everyone* who believes, for the Jew first and also for the Greek" (Romans 1:16 – NKJV).

May everyone believe in the gospel and be saved (you, too, whoever you are)!

Consider the truth which the Scriptures declare about God: He is an "impartial Judge" who judges "each one" (1 Peter 1:17). Every single person is judged by God in an *impartial* manner. Calvinism would describe God as being very partial to certain predestined individuals.

Romans 2:4–11 (NASB) says, "For *there is no partiality with God*" (v. 11). God will "render to every man" (v. 6) not on the basis of some predestination of God, but on the basis of the "righteous judgment of God" (v. 5). Why will some be judged with wrath and indignation? Because of their "stubbornness and unrepentant heart" (v. 5). Because they "do not obey the truth" (v. 8). They were invited to repent and obey (not by any merit of their own, but by the kindness of God - v. 4), but they chose to "obey unrighteousness" (v. 8).

Paul goes to many extremes throughout his letters to get this point across. Romans 3:9 (and following) puts all men in the same condition. Jews and Greeks alike are all "under sin." Romans 3:21–22 (ESV) gives the answer to the plight in which all find themselves, and that answer is "the righteousness of God!" How do I receive this? "Through faith in Jesus Christ for *all* who believe. *For there is no distinction*." This verse is falsehood if God gives some the opportunity to respond, and not others (as is promoted by Calvinism). Please notice the implicit danger to which some have fallen prey, and that being, making the same mistake the Jews made in many cases in thinking *they* were the only ones offered the kingdom.

Listen to Peter's confession in Acts 10:34–35 (ESV), "Truly I understand that *God shows no partiality*, but in every nation *anyone* who fears him and does what is right is acceptable to him."

Again, notice, "Whoever believes in Him will not be disappointed" (Romans 10:11 – NASB). Again, "Whoever will call upon the name of the Lord will be saved" (Romans 10:13 – NASB). Again, "For there is no distinction between Jew and Greek; for the same Lord is Lord of all, abounding in riches for *all* who call upon Him" (Romans 10:12 – NASB).

The very point in all this is that not just one kind or group of people can respond, and others can't, but that the gospel is indeed for *all* (you, too, *whoever* you are)!

This was God's plan from the beginning through Abraham. God said, "and all the peoples on earth will be blessed through you" (Genesis 12:3c – HCSB).

Romans 15:9–12 quotes several passages from the Old Testament, revealing God's eternal intentions concerning all peoples.

Paul develops the "mystery" of the gospel as being, "that is, how the Gentiles are fellow heirs, members of the same body, and partakers of the promise in Christ Jesus through the gospel" (Ephesians 3:6 – RSV).

The very nature of all the above passages speaks of the *inclusion of all* people in the message of the gospel. Also, how can the gospel, meaning "good news," be good news to *you*, if it's not *for* you? But praise God! It is for you and for me and for any person who will respond!

"Fear not: for, behold, I bring you good tidings of great joy, which shall be to *all* people" (Luke 2:10 – KJV).

"When they heard these things they fell silent. And they glorified God, saying, 'Then to the Gentiles also God has granted repentance that leads to life'" (Acts 11:18 – ESV).

Repent, therefore, whoever you are, and believe in the gospel!

You say, "What if I am a wicked person? What if I have done horrible things? Can I respond, too?" Certainly! Tax collectors were detestable people in the eyes of the Jews because many times they were thieves in relation to the amount of taxes they demanded. The Bible says that the tax gatherers and the harlots who responded to the preaching of John the Baptist will get into the kingdom of God (Matthew 21:31–32).

Jesus said, "Those who are well have no need of a physician, but those who are sick. But go and learn what this means: 'I desire mercy and not sacrifice.' For *I did not come to call the righteous, but sinners*, to repentance" (Matthew 9:12–13 – NKJV). If you are a sinner, you fit into the category of those Jesus came to call!

Also, in the parable of the marriage feast, the Scripture says that they went out and "gathered everyone they found, both evil and good" (Matthew 22:10 – HCSB).

Why do you suppose God "makes his sun to rise on the evil and on the good, and sends rain on the just and on the unjust" (Matthew 5:45 – ESV)? Is it not to demonstrate His true *love for all* people?

Read the *inclusive* nature of God's will in Isaiah 56:6–8 (NASB). Not only was the Lord willing for "foreigners" to "join themselves to the LORD," but He also referred to His own house by saying, "My house will be called a house of prayer for *all* the peoples" (56:7d). Do you believe God really meant this? Do you believe that God meant that there was to be a place where *anybody* could come and have close communion ("prayer") with Him? I believe it because God's Word proclaims it over and over. This is the spirit of the Word and of Christ and of the Gospel. Whoever you are, God has made the access to His throne of grace available to *you*, too!

Just in case you do not think that God was very serious about this matter of His house, let's look at what we usually call the "cleansing of the temple" in Matthew 21:12–17. Why was Jesus so bold to "cast out" those buying and selling? Because this particular place in the temple, the court of the Gentiles, was that arena where *anybody* in the world could come and seek and know the one true God. And Jesus was very upset that this avenue of life was being destroyed by those selling merchandise, so He drove them out! He wanted all people, people just like you and me, to have an avenue of faith and hope, where they could freely come to God, know Him, and relate to Him.

When the Philippian jailer asked, "Sirs, what must I do to be saved?," they did not say, "Well, we'll have to check to see if you are one of the chosen elect!" The message they had been preaching was for him, too. They said, "Believe in the Lord Jesus, and you shall be saved" (Acts 16:30–31 – NASB).

This is the message of our next chapter. God extends to you an invitation to respond to the gospel (yes, *you*, whoever you are)!

Chapter 3

I Love You! Follow Me, and
Live with Me Forever!

"Come unto me, all ye that labour and are heavy laden, and I will give you rest. Take my yoke upon you, and learn of me; for I am meek and lowly in heart: and ye shall find rest unto your souls" (Matthew 11:28–29 – KJV).

At times Jesus has been called "The Inviter." We never hear Him say, "Please, accept Me as your Lord and Savior." But we hear Him saying over and over, "*Come*, follow Me!," and as above, "*Come* unto me, all ye that labour…," and "If anyone thirsts, let him *come* to Me…"

One may say, "But isn't He inviting only His *chosen* people, not all people?" Matthew 9:9–13 expresses that Christ came *not* to call the righteous, but "sinners," like Matthew, the tax collector. Surely, with this benevolent spirit to call the sinners, tax-gatherers, and harlots, we do not find Christ coming to call just some of these wicked people (only the *elect* sinners?; the *elect* tax collectors?; the *elect* harlots?). For all have sinned! All fit into this category of people that Christ came to call! All need Him as Lord and Savior!

The Rich Young Ruler wanted eternal life (Matthew 19:16–26). Did Jesus, or did He not actually invite this man to have life when He said, ". . . come, follow Me"? If the man had heeded Christ's instructions, would he not have found "treasure in heaven"? Certainly, Jesus did extend an invitation to this man. Now those who would suggest that God only calls or invites His elect will have to work hard to say that an invitation from the Lord Jesus Christ Himself does not constitute a real call.

If Jesus, the King of Kings, invites you to follow Him, He would not at the same time prevent you from coming to Him by predestining you to hell. Would this represent His character? Would He be deceptive in this way? Of course not!

Jesus does not invite just some, and exclude everyone else. Just in case you are wondering, *you are on His invitation list*!

Notice those who were invited to the wedding feast in Matthew 22:1–14. "Go therefore to the main highways, and *as many as you find there*, invite to the wedding feast" (v. 9 – NASB). This is obviously an *all inclusive* invitation. We would in no way assume that they just happened to find only the *elect* sinners on all these "main highways." Therefore, those who did not respond (so as to be saved) did actually receive an authentic invitation to which they could have accepted had they chosen to do so. In Luke's account, they were commanded to go out and bring in the "poor and crippled and blind and lame." Those who were considered to be suffering severe conditions as a result of their own sin were also invited to the feast. Certainly we would not assume that every single person in these categories of sinners were all elect. But they all did receive the invitation!

So, we must ask the question, "Is an invitation from the Heavenly Father an invitation indeed?" Certainly, it is! They could have come if they had chosen to accept the invitation. Therefore, those who rejected the invitation did so *not* because they were predestined to do so, but because they *chose* to reject it. You do have a choice! If they had been predestined to reject it, the invitation would not be considered authentic.

When they had accomplished these invitations, they were further instructed to "Go out to the highways and hedges and compel people to come in, that my house may be filled" (Luke 14:23 – ESV). The very nature of this parable teaches that *everybody* gets invited to the marriage supper of the Lamb (the wedding feast for Christ and His Bride, the Church). We are actually "compelled" to accept the invitation. The question is, Will you respond? (see chapter 7 of this book).

What about those in the first part of the parable who refused to accept the invitation? Were these really invited? Or was this just some formality to be able to say that those who are not the elect are still responsible for rejecting the invitation? No! If our God in Christ Jesus extends you an invitation, it is real, authentic, and genuine. God cannot lie, nor is there any falsehood in Him. You can actually respond to His invitation, if you choose to do so!

Those at the beginning of the parable were indeed invited. As a matter of fact, messengers were sent more than once to extend the call. Having been invited by the messengers of the king himself, certainly, they could have come if they had so desired! Why did they not come? Because they were not predestined? No! "They were not willing to come" (Matthew 22:3 – NKJV). By an act of their own will, they clearly rejected the invitation! Also, why would the king (representing the Heavenly Father) be so furious such that he destroyed them and their city (Matthew 22:7)? If they were just doing what God had predestined them to do, the king (God) would have no need to be angry. But they indeed were dishonoring the son of the king (representing Christ) by making other matters of life higher in priority! Their response rightfully enraged the king.

He concludes with "many are called but few are chosen." The word *many* here is not a limiting word, for it is defined in the parable itself by "invite everyone you find ... both evil and good" (Matthew 22:9–10 – HCSB). And notice how then this parable defines those who are *chosen* (this is the same Greek word for the *elect*). They are defined as those who responded to the invitation, and came as requested – in proper wedding clothes (only dressed in the righteousness of Christ, not clothed in their own merit, goodness, etc.).

You are invited! Please lay aside your own righteousness, and honor with me the Son of the King, Jesus Christ. Put on His righteousness, and enjoy the feast!

Do not miss the host of admonitions and commands to have a right relationship with God. These "invitations" from God come in many different forms. For instance, "Enter by the narrow gate..." (Matthew 7:13 – RSV). Why would Jesus preach this to the multitudes if some of them really could not "enter"? Why would He offer them this path that leads to life, if they had already been predestined to hell?

Jesus said, "If anyone *wishes* to come after Me, let him deny himself, and take up his cross daily, and follow Me" (Luke 9:23 – NASB). Why would Jesus say this if men could not really respond to their "wish"? Also, "Repent: for the kingdom of heaven is at hand" (Matthew 4:17 – KJV). Why would Jesus call people to repent, if God had not given them the ability (true invitation) to do so?

He has extended a strong call to all of us to get right with Him. These calls are actually *invitations*.

"Therefore having overlooked the times of ignorance, God is now declaring to men that *all everywhere* should repent, because He has fixed a day in which He will judge the world in righteousness..." (Acts 17:30–31 – NASB). "All" and "everywhere" completely cover it! Don't you think? God's call to get right with Him is to any and every person!

God says, "Turn to Me and be saved, all the ends of the earth" (Isaiah 45:22 – NASB). Again, "all the ends of the earth" covers it! Wouldn't you agree? Also, again, how can a man turn to God if God has, through predestination, prevented him? Why do I need a warning about a day when God will judge the world? If I am predestined to be saved, I will be judged as righteous by His own foreordination. If I am predestined to go to hell, all the turning in the world won't help. But praise God, that is not the determination of the Lord. The call to "Turn...and be saved" is for you and me, too! For He issues the call to "all the ends of the earth." Every man needs this call and warning! That's why God gave it again through Paul on Mars Hill (Acts 17:30–31). The prophets had been giving it "again and again" (Jeremiah 29:19; 35:15). John the Baptist gave the warning (Matthew 3:2)! Jesus preached this message (Matthew 4:17)! And a host of preachers since then, in the name of Jesus Christ, have continued this call to all men, "Repent and be saved!"

John 1:9 (KJV) says, "That was the true Light, which lighteth every man that cometh into the world." Every man, woman, boy and girl receives an invitation from the Light of the world, Jesus Christ! You may say, "What about all those people who have never heard the name of Jesus? Do they receive an invitation?" Romans 1:18–21 makes it clear that the very character of God is revealed in creation, and that this knowledge is evident within people to the extent that when they do not respond to that knowledge, they actually are "suppressing" the truth (v. 18). So, the conclusion is that they are "without excuse," since they "knew God" (v. 21). They have no excuse for failing to honor God, for creation has told them of Him (see also Psalm 19:1–4).

I certainly must say here, aren't you glad someone came along and told you about Jesus? Let's not leave the witnessing to creation. Let's be obedient and share the excellencies of Him who called us out of darkness into His light!

"Oh, taste and see that the LORD is good! Blessed is the man who takes refuge in him" (Psalm 34:8 – ESV)!

These calls, encouragements, warnings, and "invitations," are all because God really does love you and *wants* you to know Him, have a close relationship with Him, and spend eternity with Him. This brings us to Chapter 4 which looks into the very heart of God. He *desires* for all to know Him!

Chapter 4

I Love You! I Long For You!

"O Jerusalem, Jerusalem, the one who kills the prophets and stones those who are sent to her! How often I wanted to gather your children together, as a hen gathers her chicks under her wings, but you were not willing!" (Matthew 23:37 – NKJB).

Does this not capture the heart and spirit of Christ? I beg you, please focus ever more closely as we move through these next four chapters. I have prayed that the first three chapters would have already convinced you of God's love for you (yes, *you*, whoever you are!), but I believe chapters 4–7 help to reveal further the very heart, activity, and will of God.

When you have an intense desire for something, do you not pursue it with all your resources and attain it if possible? Certainly, that is exactly what we do. What about God? Is there anything that God would want that He could not have at His finger tips? Of course, not! He created everything. He owns everything. He is in control of the universe. He has the final word in everything. So

God can have anything He wants (and, of course, we all agree that anything God would want would not compromise His character or holiness).

Do you suppose that our Lord God would have a desire for something that He Himself, before all time, would have foreordained that He could not have? Of course, not! Now understand that God has indeed determined that the lost whom He desires to save, will spend eternity in hell if they do not respond to Christ in faith. But His desire (eternal will) never was that they be saved without faith, without a true personal relationship, without forgiveness, etc.

In relation to the above passage, was Jesus really upset over Jerusalem, or was this just some "front" or "show" to make an emotional impact upon those who read the Scriptures? If He really longed for Jerusalem in this way, why did He not just predestine them to be saved from the beginning of time, and He would have been able to gather them under His wings? For Calvinism says that God does all things "for His good pleasure." Then why did He not predestine that which would please Him according to passages like this one concerning Jerusalem? If that's what He *wanted* to do, He certainly could have done such! This passage says that Jesus often "wanted" to gather them. But the text here very plainly tells us why He did not gather them: because they were "not willing." They would not, by an act of their *will*, respond to His invitation to be gathered. Therefore, Christ's desire to gather them is further qualified with the truth that His desire and plan is to gather those who willingly respond in faith. Otherwise, He could have simply forced them, through predestination, to allow Him to gather them. But that is not the will or way of God. Jesus truly wants a genuine, willing response of faith from us.

If faith is something God just "zaps" upon people in predestination so that they will respond to Him, then why did He not just do such with these people He so desired to gather? And don't say, "He couldn't gather them because He is a holy God, and they were sinners." For all of us whom He does gather are sinners! The holy God we all claim to know saves sinners only! That's the only kind of people there are to save. The reason He did not save Jerusalem is because she was "not willing" (v. 37), not because God didn't predestine her.

Listen to the heart of our God in the following passages in Jeremiah. God says, "My soul, my soul! I am in anguish! Oh, my heart!" Please carefully read Jeremiah 4:18–22 and 8:18–22 (NASB). What passion and pain we find in the heart of God as He looks upon the plight of His people in their sin and rebellion. Certainly this is not just theatrics! Certainly God has not predestined these people to hell and is now wishing He hadn't! He asks the question, "Is there no balm in Gilead? Is there no physician there?" (8:22). Certainly there was help for the Israelites! Then why were they not healed? "Because they have forsaken My law which I set before them, and have not obeyed My voice nor walked according to it" (Jeremiah 9:13 – NASB). Their plight in life was a result of their own sin, not because God didn't choose (predestine) them!

We must continue throughout our search for truth to find our answers in the very wording of Scripture, not in the wisdom or calculations of man!

Give attention to other passages that reveal the very heart and *desire* of God:

God said to Moses, "How long will this people spurn Me? And ... not believe in Me, despite all the signs which I have performed in their midst?" (Numbers 14:11 – NASB).

"Oh that they had such a mind as this always, to fear me and to keep all my commandments, that it might go well with them and with their descendants forever (Deuteronomy 5:29 – ESV)!

"Oh, that my people would listen to me, that Israel would walk in my ways! I would soon subdue their enemies and turn my hand against their foes" (Psalm 81:13–14 – ESV).

Why all this passion and longing on the part of God if He Himself is the One who dictates people's end? If God was that broken over it, why didn't He just predestine them to respond properly? Again, because that is not the way or the will of God! What God really desires is a genuine response from the heart of all people, not some robot-like, preprogrammed response. God is not playing toy soldiers!

1 Timothy 2:3–4 (NASB) says, ". . . God our Savior, ... *desires all* men to be saved and to come to the knowledge of the truth." Can this be any simpler? Can this be any clearer? Isn't it wonderful to know that this is the heart and soul of our Lord! The very desire of God is that "all men" will be saved. Are all men saved? Certainly not! Why not? Because even though the gospel is for all men (since God "desires all men to be saved"), all men do not receive it in faith. Many reject it, by an act of their own free will!

Yet *The Westminster Confession of Faith* states, "The rest of mankind *God was pleased*, according to the unsearchable counsel of His own will, whereby He extendeth or withholdeth mercy, as He pleaseth, for the glory of His sovereign power over His creatures, to pass by; and *to ordain them to dishonor and wrath* for their sin, to the praise of His glorious justice" (chapter 3, part 7).

How can anyone believe that God is "pleased" for His own glory to foreordain some men to hell, when the Bible says that God *desires* all men to be saved (1 Timothy 2:3–4)? These two statements do not line up with one another! They cannot coexist! So which will we choose to uphold: man's wisdom, or the Word of God? Let's stick with the Word!

Romans 11:32 (NASB) says, "For God has shut up all in disobedience that He might show mercy to *all*" (see also Romans 3:19, 23 and 5:20).

The teaching concerning the Law in the book of Romans reveals that God has grouped all peoples into one category: *disobedient sinners, who are accountable.* According to the above passage, His desire is to "show mercy to *all.*"

This means He desires to show mercy to me and to you (yes, *you*, whoever you are!).

Matthew 18:14 (HCSB) says, "It is not the will of your Father in heaven that one of these little ones perish." Notice here the emphatic pointing to even "one." Notice the searching concern of God in this text over any one who strays (straying sheep used to be killed by wild animals). God really cares for you. He really cares for me. There is not one He does not love! There is not one He *wills* to be devoured by Satan, the roaring lion! That's why Jesus came, "to seek and to save that which was lost" (Luke 19:10 – KJV). Are you lost? If so, He came for you.

2 Corinthians 4:4 (NASB) says, "...the god of this world has blinded the minds of the unbelieving, that they might not see the light of the gospel..." The obvious implication of this passage is that were it not for the work of Satan, the "unbelieving" might see the gospel and believe. Calvinism would lead us to believe that it is really God who has blinded (or "not opened") their minds through predestination. This gives God the credit for the work of Satan, the evil tempter. "Let no one say when he is tempted, 'I am being tempted by God'; for God cannot be tempted by evil, and He Himself does not tempt anyone" (James 1:13 – NASB). Also, if Calvinism is true, why would Satan need to worry about blinding the minds of those who have already been predestined to hell? That part of his work would be useless, for they would already be eternally blind.

1 Corinthians 6:13 (RSV) says, "Food is meant for the stomach and the stomach for food... The body is not meant for immorality, but for the Lord, and the Lord for the body." Why did God create us? For what purpose is our body? According to this passage,

our bodies were created for the Lord, and not for immorality. Calvinism would lead us to believe that God created our bodies, and yet some of us cannot receive the Lord by the very mandate of the Lord through predestination. Why would God create our bodies to house the Lord, and then dictate that some of our bodies could not receive Him (that we could not have the opportunity to fulfill the very purpose for which we were created)? He would not do such!

Man was created to have fellowship with God, to know Him. Why would we encourage all people to fulfill their created purpose, if some are not even given the option to pursue that purpose? If predestination means that God *wills* some to eternal life and others to eternal damnation, then those predestined to damnation do not even have the opportunity to fulfill their purpose. That would mean that God created some men for a purpose that He Himself does not allow them to have the opportunity to fulfill.

What about people Calvinists say are predestined to heaven? Why would they need to strive to know God if God is going to automatically give that life to them anyway? But He doesn't automatically set us right! His call from one end of the Bible to the other is to *choose* to get right! We must personally respond to God in faith!

God tells Ezekiel to say to His people, "As I live!" declares the Lord God, "I take no pleasure in the death of the wicked, but rather that the wicked turn from his way and live. Turn back, turn back from your evil ways! Why then will you die, O house of Israel?" (Ezekiel 33:11 – NASB). How can we not clearly hear the heart of God in this text? The Calvinist doctrine declares that "it pleased God to damn some . . .," but that is very specifically anti-scriptural. God takes "no pleasure in the death of the wicked." Very specifically, that which would please God is for the wicked to turn (repent) and live. This is the will of God! God would not *will* (desire) for the wicked to turn and *live*, while at the same time having already *willed* (predestined) the wicked to *die*.

When the wicked die and go to hell, who are those people? According to Calvinists, they are those whom the Lord predestined to go there. But according to the Word of God, they are people that God would "rather" they had turned and lived! The very wording of this text (what it *says*) clearly implies that God's will for them was not eternal condemnation, but eternal life. His will was that they "turn" and "live!" It clearly implies that they had opportunity to respond, for that was the very desire of God.

If we disagree with what the Bible *says*, then we might as well construct any god we choose, who handles his business in any way we design. But praise God, we also hear His very heart in the end of the text with, "Turn back... Why will you die, O house of Israel?" Do you hear God's heart? Do you hear His cry? Upon asking, "Why will you die?", would He catch Himself with, "Oh, I forgot! I predestined you to hell!"? Of course, not!

God had warned them (Ezekiel 33:7). The very nature of a warning is that upon hearing it, you have the opportunity to take heed and get right. Why, then, did they not turn back? Because their way was not right (33:17, 20), and they refused to do what God was calling them to do through Ezekiel (33:30–33).

When a wicked man does get right, why does he do so? If you follow the parallel passage in Ezekiel 18, you find that he turned, not because God forced him, but because he "considered" and turned (18:28).

Why do you suppose Jesus has not come back yet? It has to do with His desire to see *all* people have the opportunity for salvation.

2 Peter 3:9 (NASB) says, "The Lord is not slow about His promise, as some count slowness, but is patient toward you, *not wishing* for *any* to perish but for *all* to come to repentance." God desires ("wishes") that none perish, but that all repent and find everlasting life.

This is the very desire and heart of God. We must not accept a theology or doctrine that denies this truth. We must not accept a belief that demands that the very wording of the holy Scriptures be denied or changed. Calvinists say that God was pleased to condemn some men to eternal damnation. The Bible says that God does not wish "for *any* to perish but for *all* to come to repentance." Again, let's stick with the Word!

God's desire for all men to be saved is so strong that He sent His only Son to die that all might live! This brings us to our next chapter which highlights the cross of our Lord and Savior, Jesus Christ.

CHAPTER 5

I LOVE YOU! JUST LOOK AT THE CROSS!

"For there is one God, and one mediator also between God and men, the man Christ Jesus, who gave Himself as *a ransom for all*, the testimony borne at the proper time" (1 Timothy 2:5–6 – NASB).

What is the true essence of the cross? Is this indeed a legal purchase agreement to justify God's bringing certain chosen people to heaven, people whom He has predestined to go there? Or is the cross not truly the most glorious act of love and sacrifice, "a ransom for all" who would choose to place their faith in Christ Jesus? The Word of God says He died for *all*!

We know love by looking at the cross. "By this we know love, that he laid down his life for us" (1 John 3:16 – ESV). When we experience the love of Jesus who has died for us, it encourages us to have faith in Him and trust Him with our lives. He died to pay the price for our sins, a price we would otherwise have to pay.

One may ask, "What is faith? Is it not a gift from God?" We must be careful here! If we define faith as something that God does in us to *move us automatically* to respond to Him, we will betray its use in Scripture. All throughout the Word of God, *faith* is very specifically used as *man's trusting response* to God's grace (a choice of his own free will). Then and only then does salvation follow. *Faith, trust, belief,* etc. become what I call "non-words" in Calvinism. They lose the essence of their scriptural use in the Calvinist's concept of predestination.

What about the cross? If God's grace is pushed upon us (forced, "irresistible"), then what is the true essence of the cross? Does it not become much less than that wonderful, amazing, loving grace proclaimed in Scripture, falling from the forefront of our faith, to be overshadowed by a show of power which is enforced only upon certain people? Does the cross then not become less love and more transaction, where the compulsion of God forces men into salvation? We know *compulsion* is not that which God desires according to 2 Corinthians 9:7. If God loves cheerful givers because it is a sincere attitude from the heart which truly blesses Him, then God is not rejoicing in something He forced upon us. He loves to see people freely choose to offer themselves to Him.

Do we not greatly offend God if we say that the act of the cross is not enough to evoke a response of love back from us without His having to force that response on us through predestination? The Scripture says, "Do you not know that it is the kindness of God that leads you to repentance?" (Romans 2:4 – NASB). Also, "I beseech you therefore, brethren, *by the mercies of God…*" (Romans 12:1 – KJV). In other words, one's choice to repent and to present his body a living sacrifice is from a willingness to do so, having considered the kindness and mercy of God, not from a preprogrammed response as conceptualized in Calvinism. Is that not why God stands in judgment against those who have not responded positively to His Son (John 3:18), holding them accountable for their rejection (see chapter 8 of this book)?

The whole "indescribable gift" of the cross becomes a candy-coating with predestination. The question then would arise, "Why did Jesus have to die on the cross for me?" In other words, if God predestined me to go to heaven, what could change that? We would all agree that when God decides something, *nothing* changes or thwarts that decision. Therefore, if God predestined me to heaven, what true purpose or essence or effect does the cross then have? Certainly an essence skewed from what we find in the Word. Also, if I do not have the capacity to respond in faith with freedom of choice, then the cross is not much concern of mine, for I cannot respond to it anyway.

One may say that the cross is the method God chose to use to justify a holy God saving sinners. Therefore, it shows the love and sacrifice of the Father to prepare you for heaven. I must ask to that comment, "Love for just me?" What about my neighbor whom the Lord has called me to love? Did the Lord love him enough to die for him, too?" One may answer, "If he is chosen!" Do you mean God called me to love my neighbor (which according to Luke 10:29–37 is any and every person), and yet He may not love my neighbor? God forbid! He indeed died for (loves) *everyone* (Hebrews 2:9).

The whole focus throughout Scripture on calling man to turn from sin becomes wasted breath if men do not actually have a choice in the matter. The dynamics of holding us accountable for sin and of calling us to repent and respond to the good news of the cross of Christ become robot-like motions in Calvinism. This reduces the message of the cross to being nothing more than the letter-head on one's ticket of predestination rather than Christ's very signature and love for any person who receives in faith Him who has died to cleanse all his sins.

The Scriptures confirm that Jesus indeed came "to seek and to save that which was lost" (not simply to affect the salvation of the elect). Who are the *lost* that Jesus came to save? Every person falls within this category (Romans 3:9, 19, 23).

Are not all unbelievers lost? Certainly, all people come into this world lost! Has anyone ever been born saved? Has anyone, other than Christ Himself, been born perfect and continued therein? Certainly not! If we are *all* born lost, and Christ came to seek the lost, then whom does He not seek? He indeed seeks *all*! And if Jesus seeks *all*, then the cross was for *everybody* (that's you, too!) Jesus said, "I have come into the world as light, so that whoever believes in me may not remain in darkness. If anyone hears my words and does not keep them, I do not judge him; for I did not come to judge the world but to save the world" (John 12:46–47 – ESV).

This is the very reason Jesus came, not to save a few particular people, but "to save *the world*." He came to offer light to those in darkness. That includes every person who has ever lived, for all who are without Him dwell in darkness! And Jesus offered us that light by dying on the cross that we might be delivered from the "domain of darkness" (Colossians 1:13).

"And *He died for all*, that they who live should no longer live for themselves, but for Him who died and rose again on their behalf" (2 Corinthians 5:15 – NASB). Notice the Scriptures never say, "He died for just some." Yes, they proclaim that He died for the Church, His Bride, but they *never* say He did not die for certain people! "But we do see Him who has been made for a little while lower than the angels, namely, Jesus, because of the suffering of death crowned with glory and honor, that by the grace of God He might taste death for *everyone*" (Hebrews 2:9 – NASB).

"In this the love of God was manifested toward us, that God has sent His only begotten Son into the world, that we might live through Him" (1 John 4:9 – NKJV). Did Jesus come to save the *elect* sinners only? No! He came into the world and truly died for all sinners, desiring all sinners to be saved (see again chapter 4 of this book)!

Romans 5:6-10 tells us that Christ died for the helpless, ungodly sinners who were His enemies. Who does this leave out? For whom did He not die? The perfect un-elect people? Certainly not (since there are no such persons)! He died for all! For all fall into the categories of *helpless, ungodly, sinners,* and *enemies.* The very fact that He died for us while in this condition, points to His love and compassion for all, not to an arbitrary choice of some wicked people over other wicked people. Indeed, the cross is the greatest proof that God really loves you, yes, *you,* whoever you are!

When Jesus said, "Father, forgive them..." (Luke 23:34), for whom was He making this request? He was speaking for all the people who were crucifying Him, all those surrounding Calvary. Were all these nailing Jesus to the cross the elect? Was the angry mob who said, "Crucify, crucify..." all elect? Were those who mocked him all elect? Were there any non-elect people surrounding the events of Calvary? In other words, were there any people surrounding the cross who would end up not saved? Certainly there were! When Jesus said, "Father, forgive them...," He was asking forgiveness for every person surrounding the cross (that represents all people). He was paying the price for the sin of all people. He was making salvation available to all people. Otherwise, He would have had to say, "Father, forgive just that one, and that one there, that one here, oh, yes, and that one over there..."

No, I tell you, the cross was indeed for every person! God's very own Word declares it! God loves you! He died for you! You can trust this is true!

Calvinism reduces the cross of Christ from its pinnacle point in God's Word to relative insignificance, being replaced by the wisdom of man in his meager attempt to defend the sovereignty of God. We would do well to abandon our own wisdom and return to knowing nothing, "except Jesus Christ, and Him crucified" (1 Corinthians 2:2)!

God in Christ Jesus was willing to humble (limit) Himself in the incarnation. When we desert or distort the Scriptures, we diminish the very name of the One we claim as Lord. Can you imagine standing before God with a group of people saying, "Almighty

Sovereign, we recognize what You said in Your word, but You really didn't say it right. For we know Jesus could not have possibly died for *the whole world*. He didn't really *tasted death for everyone*. He certainly was not *a ransom for all*. So we changed it, because we believe that Jesus was the propitiation for our sins *only*! We hope You don't mind us putting the cross of Christ, the death of Your only begotten Son, a little lower than where You had it!" This is what the Calvinist doctrine truly implies. Calvinism does not accept how God verbalizes truth in His own Word. But, praise the Lord, God's wisdom and Word is completely sufficient, and God is no liar!

1 Timothy 1:15 (ESV) says, "The saying is trustworthy and deserving of full acceptance, that Christ Jesus came into the world to save sinners, of whom I am the foremost." This brings us to our next chapter, where we are called to seek out (evangelize and disciple) all people by persuading them to fully accept the truth that Jesus came to save sinners. Paul's own persuasion here is, "If He saved me, the greatest sinner, He will save you, too" (for He died for all sinners)! Christ died for you, me, and the whole world. He died a death of substitution in the place of sinners. Accept by faith His love and forgiveness shared for you in the cross!

Chapter 6

I Love You! My Disciples Are Seeking You!

"Go ye therefore, and teach all nations, baptizing them in the name of the Father, and of the Son, and of the Holy Ghost: Teaching them to observe all things whatsoever I have commanded you: and, lo, I am with you alway, even unto the end of the world. Amen" (Matthew 28:19–20 – KJV).

"But you shall receive power when the Holy Spirit has come upon you; and you shall be my witnesses in Jerusalem and in all Judea and Samaria and to the end of the earth" (Acts 1:8 – RSV).

Praise the Lord that when He sends out His messengers with the Gospel, that this wonderful news is for you, for me, and for every single person on the planet.

Speaking of John the Baptist, John 1:7 (HCSB) says, "He came as a witness to testify about the light, so that *all* might believe through him." Can you imagine the joy that flooded the heart of John the Baptist? He had been preaching as the forerunner of Christ, calling people to repent, and telling them about the coming Messiah. Then, appearing through the crowd, there He was, and John had the thrill of personally pointing out the Lord Jesus Christ! He said, "Behold, the Lamb of God who takes away the sin of the world!" (John 1:29 – NASB). What a statement! What an introduction! What a relief to have delivered the message, expressed the truth, and heralded the promise. And there stood the *Truth* and the *Promise* in the Person of Jesus Christ. Yet what a heart break to know that there are some who would reduce that incredible introduction at the Jordan River to, "Hey guys, look, there's Jesus, who takes away the sin of some of us!" Oh, listen, if that were the case, those for whom He did not die would have to look for another Messiah, another Savior. But, friends, there is only One! "For there is one God, and one mediator also between God and men, the man Christ Jesus, who gave Himself as a ransom for *all*" (1 Timothy 2:5–6 – NASB).

In the parable that Jesus told of the slaves going out to invite people to the wedding feast, they went out and "gathered together *all they found*" (Matthew 22:10 – NASB). We notice that in the multitude of passages like these, we are never limited in seeking only the *elect* or *chosen*, but we are called to seek out all people that they might receive the gospel. "Go therefore to the main highways, and *as many as you find there*, invite to the wedding feast" (Matthew 22:9 – NASB).

Paul spoke in this light of his mission in Christ when he said, "through whom we have received grace and apostleship to bring about the obedience of faith for the sake of his name among *all* the nations" (Romans 1:5 – ESV).

Paul said, "For we must all appear before the judgment seat of Christ... Knowing, therefore, the terror of the Lord, we persuade men" (2 Corinthians 5:10–11 – NKJV). Why would Paul spend time trying to "persuade men" to do that which they were not predestined to do? He would have never wasted his time doing this if he had believed men did not have a choice. One may say, "Paul did not know which ones were the elect." Still then, if they had been predestined to heaven, they would not need persuading.

Also, God has not called us into a cat and mouse game where we invite persons to salvation in Christ Jesus, all along wondering if God actually is willing to offer them His grace! Should we, on behalf of God, offer someone something from Him, when God Himself has not offered it to them? Is that not deceit? Is that not a lie? "God is light, and in him is no darkness at all" (1 John 1:5 – ESV)! God cannot lie (Titus 1:2)! Should we, on God's behalf, offer a lie? May it never be!

Why would Paul have such a strong desire and fervent prayer for the salvation of his brethren (Romans 9:1–3 and 10:1) if he believed in predestination? Why would he pray for that which had already been predetermined before all time, knowing that his prayer would have absolutely no impact on their opportunity or response?

Paul said, "I have great sorrow and unceasing grief in my heart. For I could wish that I myself were accursed... for the sake of my brethren" (Romans 9:2–3 – NASB). My goodness, did Paul love those people more than God did? Of course, not! But it cannot be said that God loved them if He did not even give them the opportunity to be saved. According to this text, Paul would have chosen for himself to be separated from Christ if it would have meant salvation for his brethren. Again, did Paul love them more than Christ did? No! That's what Christ did for all men! He bore the penalty of being "accursed" for all men that all might be saved! Jesus is the source from which Paul attained his attitude and spirit toward these people who were lost.

It is quite evident throughout the whole of Scripture that we, the disciples, witnesses, and children of God, are to love all people. Has God asked us to do something that He has not done? Certainly not! We are to love *all* and pursue *all* with the gospel for the sake of Jesus Christ, for He Himself loves all!

If Paul had believed in predestination, he would have never said, "if by any means I may provoke *to jealousy* those who are my flesh and save some of them" (Romans 11:14 – NKJV). For Paul would have known that the method of jealousy would have absolutely no impact on what God had already decided in predestination.

What about our dear children? When you share Jesus with your own children, do you believe that they have the option (the choice) to respond to Christ? If you are a Calvinist, how do you know God predestined them? You don't! Some believe that the children of Christians are predestined by God to salvation. Not only do our experiences in life and recent history show us that some strong Christians have children who reject Christ, but we also find in the Scriptures examples of such [Eli's sons, who did not know the Lord (1 Samuel 2:12), also, there were kings who did right in the sight of the Lord who had sons who became kings, who did evil in the sight of the Lord (Jehoram - 2 Chronicles 21:1–6).].

Our joy is that our children have the same opportunity as others, knowing Jesus died for them, too. Also, we rejoice that His disciples are out sharing that good news, news we pray will reach our children when they are in seasons of life in which they refuse to listen to us.

Yet *The Westminster Confession of Faith* says, "Elect infants, dying in infancy, are regenerated, and saved by Christ, through the Spirit, who worketh... how He pleaseth... Others, not elected... *cannot be saved*" (chapter 10, parts 3 & 4).

If you believe Calvinists, there is no hope for your children, other than *hoping* God predestined them before all time. But praise God for the truth of the Word of God, that "*whosoever* shall call upon the name of the Lord shall be saved" (Romans 10:13 – KJV)!

What a joy it is to offer the gospel to all men, knowing that this is indeed the message of the Scriptures. 2 Corinthians 5:18–21 (NASB) makes it very clear that as ambassadors for Christ, our ministry of reconciliation is to share the fact that "God was in Christ reconciling *the world* to Himself." Is God, or is He not, actually "entreating through us" men to be reconciled to Himself (2 Corinthians 5:20)? According to this passage, we are to "beg" men to get right with God. Again, is God offering a lie to some men through His ambassadors? Calvinists believe that some of the world have been predestined to hell, and therefore cannot be reconciled no matter how much we beg. If that is true, when we beg this portion of men to be reconciled to God, we are offering them a lie on behalf of God! Is this how we are to represent God? Is God entreating through us a lie when we witness to some men? Certainly not! "God *was* in Christ, reconciling *the world* to Himself! Each person is and can be invited with all honesty and truth!

I will not be accused of treating the cross as trivial. God is not just playing "toy soldiers." Yet, those who teach predestination cause the gospel, the good news about Jesus dying for us on the cross, the greatest act of love and sacrifice ever shared, to become a note of trivia in an overall plan of predestination, rather than the "power of God to salvation for everyone who believes" (Romans 1:16 – NKJV). Indeed the gospel of the cross is the only route to salvation by grace through faith made available to every man. Each man is called to make a choice, that choice being spelled out continually throughout God's Word in a vast amount of different calls, warnings, commands, and admonitions.

Jesus is never heard excluding from His message those who were not the elect. Notice, in speaking to the Jews who were trying to kill Him (John 5:18), men who were obviously not saved, Jesus shares some very specific truths with them and then says, "I say these things so that you may be saved" (John 5:34 – ESV). Now did Jesus not know that these men were not the elect? For why would He be hoping to see them saved, if He had already, from the beginning of time, predestined that they could not be saved? But that was not the case. Jesus was giving them the opportunity to respond to Him in faith by an act of their own will. Jesus shared the gospel even with those who were against Him, because He really did love each person and sought to evangelize all, that they might turn and find salvation in Him.

Jesus came to call sinners to repentance (Luke 5:32). The disciples of Jesus are to take up His mission as the Body of Christ. We, as His children, are to call sinners. Paul even expressed the extent to which he went to offer the gospel in 1 Corinthians 9:22 (NASB) when he said, "I have become all things to all men, that I may by all means save some." If men were already predestined (or not predestined) to respond to the gospel, this effort would have been unnecessary, and Paul would not have used it, knowing it was useless. Sharing the gospel is futility in Calvinism. For if God predestined men to salvation, there would be no need to strive to build a relationship with people to convince them to respond to the gospel, for God would have already seen to their response through the foreordination of their lives (and, of course, in those predestined to hell, He would have seen to it that they could not respond to the encouragement of a witness).

But God *has* given each man the ability to accept or to reject the gospel. This brings us to the next chapter which speaks of the free will that man has been given to respond to Christ. God holds us accountable for making that choice!

"…these are written that you may believe that Jesus is the Christ, the Son of God, and that believing you may have life in His name" (John 20:31 – NKJV).

CHAPTER 7

I LOVE YOU! LOVE ME!

"So *choose* life in order that you may live, you and your descendants, by loving the LORD your God, by obeying His voice, and by holding fast to Him; for this is your life" (Deuteronomy 30:19–20 – NASB).

From the beginning, man has been called to make the *choice* to properly respond to God. Multitudes of passages similar to that above call us to respond to God by loving Him, being devoted to Him, and by serving Him faithfully. These verses very emphatically imply that God has given us the free choice to accept His call or to reject it. Just in the book of Deuteronomy, see verses like 6:5; 10:20; 13:4; etc.

This choice, in a major sense, is that which we call *faith* or placing our faith and trust in God. Faith is a very real response that is made by man utilizing his own free will to react positively to God's grace. Romans 5:2 (NASB) says, "through whom also we have obtained our introduction *by faith* into this grace in which we stand." We stand, not on our faith, but on God's grace. But our movement into that grace is our own personal faith, a free choice (see also, Romans 4:12, 16).

I do not deny that it all begins with God, is enabled by God, and is compelled by God. But I declare that He (yes, in His *sovereignty*) gives us a choice, and we must exercise faith! Some would say this faith is an instilling within us from God to move toward Him in a positive response, and that it has nothing to do with our own decision or will.

For instance, *The Westminster Confession of Faith* states (chapter 10, part 2), "This effectual call is of God's free and special grace alone, not from anything at all foreseen in *man, who is altogether passive therein, until, being quickened and renewed by the Holy Spirit*, he is thereby enabled to answer this call, and to embrace the grace offered and conveyed in it." In other words, Calvinism deduces that we do not respond to Christ in faith until *after* the Lord "quickens" us (saves us, regenerates us, etc.).

But the Bible says in Romans 3:26, 28 that those who have faith in Christ are those who are justified (not: those who get justified, then subsequently exercise faith). John 1:12 does not say that when God gives us power (regenerates us), we then receive Christ. But it declares that when we receive Christ ("believe in His name"), we *then* receive power to become His children.

Notice, it is very clear, that the Holy Spirit is given "*after* believing in the Lord Jesus Christ" (Acts 11:17 – NASB). Our response of faith is necessary b*efore* salvation is given. Also, *turning* "from darkness to light" and from "Satan to God" clearly *precedes* "forgiveness of sins" (Acts 26:17–18 – ESV).

In Acts 2:37-38 (ESV), we find people having heard the gospel, being convicted in their hearts (by the Holy Spirit, yes, as He initiates the communication of truth), saying, "What shall we do?" The response is not: "Wait to see if you're predestined, for if so, it will come to you.", but "Repent and be baptized every one of you... for the forgiveness of your sins," (repentance is *before* forgiveness) and *then* "you will receive the gift of the Holy Spirit" (not before!). This is the message of the Bible from one end to the other. Man is to choose to turn away from sin, so that he can receive salvation in Christ.

Peter says, "As the *outcome* of your faith you obtain the salvation of your souls" (1 Peter 1:9 – RSV). The word *outcome* here confirms that faith comes *before* salvation. Salvation is the *result* ("outcome") of faith in Christ according to this passage. You must choose to receive (trust) or to reject (disbelieve) the grace and salvation that God offers you!

This is God's purpose for all mankind! As Paul speaks under the moving of the Holy Spirit, he mentions "every nation of men...on all the face of the earth" (Acts 17:26 – NKJV). Now, that indeed is *everybody*! He then very clearly mentions a purpose for all: "so that they should seek the Lord, in the hope that they might grope for Him and find Him" (Acts 17:27 – NKJV). The Word of God states here that this is a purpose for all mankind. If God is saying that a general purpose or pursuit for all persons is to seek Him, then indeed He will make it possible for us to find Him when we do seek Him. How can this possibly be a purpose for all mankind, if God has, before all time, prevented some men from doing such? Such would not be the ordination of our God! He would not give a purpose to all men, and then prevent some men from fulfilling the very purpose He Himself gave them. Indeed, you and I (and every person) should seek Him while He may be found (Isaiah 55:6). And, praise the Lord, we will most certainly find Him, when we seek Him with all our heart (Jeremiah 29:13)!

If my seeking, repenting, believing, etc. is some rigged, predestined thing, then are we not saying that God did not think He was wonderful enough to evoke a response of love from man? Does that not imply that people would not actually respond to God positively on their own, such that He had to force some of us through predestination to repent, to believe in Him, to obey Him, to fear Him, and to honor Him? I do not believe that this life, this kingdom of God, is that trivial. I do not believe that the Father who humbled Himself to being a servant in the incarnation, who took the humility of the cross for the likes of us, would have then robotized people into believing Him, and then acted like He was actually receiving some glory and praise from them, since they would just be doing what He programmed them to do.

Was this not the very case with Job? What was Satan's complaint? Was it not that God had provided such a hedge around Job that the only reason Job honored God was because God had set Job up so well that Job had no other natural response but to fear and honor God? Satan was saying that if Job had another set of circumstances, he would respond differently (Job 1:9–11). But God allowed Job to be tested to prove that Job's honor of God was genuine (the kind of response God desires in us, rather than a forced response). When Job's good fortune was removed, Job still honored God, because Job had true faith in God and had chosen to honor Him regardless of his circumstances in life. He rejoiced "in unsparing pain" that he had not "denied the words of the Holy One" (Job 6:10 – NASB). He also said, "Though He slay me, I will hope in Him" (Job 13:15 – NASB).

Satan would have never challenged Job's integrity if God had preprogrammed (*predestined*) Job to honor Him. Satan thought he had the chance to get Job to make the *choice* to curse God to His face (Job 1:11). Unless Satan knew that Job had a free choice in the matter of being faithful to God, he would have never accepted the challenge to test Job's faith. So praise God, Job is a true example of those who *choose* to have faith in God, when he could have chosen to "curse God and die" as his wife encouraged him to do (Job 2:9 – NKJV). Job truly brought honor to God!

This is the kind of response that has always been pleasing to God. 2 Corinthians 9:6–7 makes it clear that God desires people who give cheerfully. In other words, having freely chosen to express their dedication and appreciation for God and His blessings, they serve Him through giving from the heart. Does God want less of a response from us in relation to salvation, in response to His love shared for us on the cross? Certainly not! He desires that we freely choose to love Him as is His admonition in Deuteronomy 30:19–20. This is our response to His having loved us first with His wonderful *agape* love!

Hosea 6:6 (HCSB) says that God desires "loyalty." How can we be truly loyal without the free choice to do so? If I am predestined to respond in a certain way, my response would be considered *as programmed*. It certainly would not be labeled as *loyalty*.

Psalm 32:9 (NASB) says, "Do not be as the horse or as the mule which have no understanding, whose trappings include bit and bridle to hold them in check. Otherwise they will not come near to you." God wants us to freely respond to His love and follow Him. Calvinism implies that we can only be like the horse or mule, that we can only come to God with the trappings of predestination. This is the very opposite of what God calls us to be in this psalm. Calvinists very clearly believe that if we were not predestined to respond to God, we would never come near to Him. Yet this passage very clearly commands us to come to God without being forced to do so. Certainly God is the one who "instructs and counsels" us (Psalm 32:8), for we do not know how to live or where to go on our own. But our response to His guidance is clearly to be from a willing choice.

In speaking of the Kingdom of God as a tree in Romans 11, Paul answers the question as to why some branches were broken off, and others grafted in. The answer is not because of God's predestining some and not others, but because of the differing responses that people exercise using their free choice. "They were broken off because of their *unbelief*, but you stand fast through *faith*" (Romans 11:20 – ESV). Why did some exercise unbelief, and others faith? Because of their own personal "acceptance" or "rejection" (Romans 11:15). These were two options of life that Paul considered still available to Israel.

And notice, if you are inclined to use Romans 9–11 as proof text for Calvinism, Paul says the Gentiles would have been "cut off" if they did not "continue" to trust in the kindness of God. Also, the Jews would be "grafted" back in, if they did not continue in their unbelief (Romans 11:22–23 – NASB). In other words, God's design from the beginning has been conditioned upon the response of man. If He had predestined things to be such that our response had nothing to do with it, then there would be no reason for an admonition concerning "continuing in His kindness," for that would be a given. No person's "continuing" (or discontinuing in unbelief) would have any impact on their standing in Christ. Yet, these passages make it clear that Gentiles and Jews are called to continue in their faith (or discontinue in their unbelief), a persistence (or alteration as it may be) that would be out of their control if their stance in Christ were already settled by predestination. Therefore, the call to continue or discontinue would be totally unfounded. It would be totally useless. These verses imply that our personal commitment (choice) has an impact on our stance in Christ, whereas in Calvinism, it has none.

You say, "How can God's love be unconditional if there is a condition concerning man's response? Unconditional love is such that we can do absolutely nothing to earn, deserve, merit, or work for it! Also, it is unconditional in the sense that God shows "no partiality" for there is "no distinction" with God. He is not a "respecter of persons." He will not offer it to just some, showing them partiality over others. The condition is simply that we must receive His love to have the relationship. We must trust Him. This condition is set forth from one end of the Bible to the other. His love is indeed unconditional. He offers it to us freely (it costs us nothing)! The relationship is conditioned upon our response to His unconditional love, our faith *in Him.*

If we begin defining the response of faith as a work, we will indeed, as does the Calvinist, conclude that faith comes after regeneration since "by works of the law no human being will be justified in his sight" (Romans 3:20 – ESV). For we believe that works come after regeneration as a natural part of the life of the born again believer. Works are not a way to salvation. But the Scriptures do not define faith as a work. Please read Romans 4:13–16. It is quite clear here that *faith in the grace* of God is seen as the antithesis (or the opposite avenue for salvation seekers) of the *works of the Law.* If the Law is the avenue for salvation, faith is made void (Romans 4:14). Verse 16 says, "For this reason it is by faith, that it might be in accordance with grace." In other words, salvation is not obtained by the works of the Law, but by faith in God's grace. The Jews were trying to get to God through the Law, and their effort in that avenue was their own personal works. But we know the only way we can get to God is by His grace, and our connection to that avenue is our own personal faith. This passage of Scripture very clearly shows that faith is not a work. Faith (believing, trusting in God) is *not* a way to earn one's salvation, it is the way to respond to the "promise" of God's grace found in Christ (rather than attempting to get to God through the works of the Law).

Jeremiah 36:3 (NASB) says, "Perhaps the house of Judah will hear all the calamity which I plan to bring on them, in order that every man will turn from his evil way; then I will forgive their iniquity and their sin." Why would God say "perhaps" this will get them to turn, if He already predestined them to respond in a certain way? Yet, the nature of Scripture through and through is that of God waiting for man to respond that He might forgive his sin (see also, Jeremiah 26:3).

Read Romans 3:22–28. Man is justified "by faith." How does this faith come? Calvinists would say God just instills it within us. No! "So then faith comes by hearing, and hearing by the word of God" (Romans 10:17 – NKJV). If you are inclined to say that it's the Word of God that ignites faith once upon hearing, then why did those who hear not receive it (Romans 10:18–21)? Because having a choice, they chose to reject it in their stubbornness and disobedience.

Remember the Rich Young Ruler! Jesus offered the man life with Him by the invitation, "…come, follow Me" (Matthew 19:21). The man, truly seeking what he must do to have eternal life (Matthew 19:16), went away sorrowful, rejecting Christ's offer, choosing to hold on to his worldly possessions.

Jesus, speaking to many of the Jews, spoke that they might be saved (John 5:34), but they were unwilling to move toward Christ and receive eternal life (John 5:40). These *chose* to reject His Word. If they had been willing to choose to come to Him, they would have been saved.

In the book of Proverbs, God offers His wisdom, but many "refused" and "ignored" His counsel (1:24–25 – ESV), "and did not *choose* the fear of the LORD" (1:29 – ESV).

You may be reading all of this thinking, "I've just always thought that God, since He's God, can do anything with us that He desires. If He decides you're going to heaven, you're going! If He decides to sentence you to hell for eternity because of your sin, He is righteous in doing so! He has the right! He's the Potter, we're the clay, and we simply have no say-so in the matter."

Well, Jehovah, the Ancient of Days, *is* sovereign! Do not deny that! But also do not deny the *words* of the Holy One! Not only can and will He do whatever He chooses to do, but also, He will be true to His Word. And in His Word, He has told us that our response to Him is critical in what He chooses to do in His sovereignty. For example, in the passage about the Potter, Calvinists would use Jeremiah 18:5–7 to express their belief concerning the sovereignty of God. *Great*! But notice God's own criteria for how He manages His sovereignty. He is not haphazard in what He does (Read Jeremiah 18:5–11).

"If that nation against which I have spoken turns from its evil, I will relent concerning the calamity I planned to bring on it" (Jeremiah 18:8 – NASB). Notice the definitive promise in the words, "...I will..." Since God cannot lie, He would not have made this declaration if He had already predestined the eternal destiny of these people (if He had predetermined not to enable them to have faith). God promises here that if men repent, then He will change what He has spoken in relation to them. The criterion for God's sovereign activity was based upon man's response or behavior.

So again, if God had predestined them, He could not have at the same time made this promise, for their eternity would be settled such that no adjustment in behavior or change of heart would alter anything. And for those who would say, "This passage is about an entire nation, and not individuals," check the concluding admonition in verse 11 which calls each individual to repent. God's desire is to bless you! Yes, *you*, whoever you are! He has a wonderful purpose for your life! Don't reject it! Repent and turn to God through Jesus Christ.

"If your right hand makes you stumble, cut it off, and throw it from you; for it is better for you that one of the parts of your body perish, than for your whole body to go into hell" (Matthew 5:30 – NASB). Cut off your hand? Why? Because it would be better to complete earthly life with one hand and go to heaven, than to go into hell with both! This implies that *my* decision to abandon the path of sin has an eternal impact on my life. Why would this passage be here if cutting off my hand (drastically turning away from sin) would not change anything in relation to my eternal destiny? In other words, there would be no reason to cut off my hand if I am not "enabled" to go to heaven. How many of us stumble (sin)? All of us! The plea therefore is for all of us. There would be no reason to make this plea if our eternity has already been settled (like so many other pleas all throughout the Bible which become insignificant and useless in Calvinism).

For instance, to whom was Christ speaking in Luke 13:3 (NKJV) when He said, "I tell you, no; but unless you repent you will *all* likewise perish"? If it were to those Calvinists say were predestined to heaven, then why would Jesus say they would perish, too, knowing they could not possibly perish? If it were to those Calvinists say were not predestined to heaven, why would Jesus give them the impression that He was calling them to repent and be saved, when He Himself would have known that was not possible? But the truth is, while some believed that certain people were greater sinners than others, Jesus placed all sinners in the same condition here. They all needed to repent. Each person must choose to turn away from his sin (repent), if he is to be right with God. And the calls of Christ give the obvious implication that each person has the opportunity to do just that.

Hebrews 12:14 (NKJV) says, "Pursue ... holiness, without which no one will see the Lord." Why would we be admonished to "pursue" holiness if salvation is not even available to us? Conversely, why would we be called to pursue holiness if it is going to be automatically given to us?

In Luke 14:16–20, were all these people not actually invited? Could they not have come if they had chosen to come? If they had come, would they not have been able to enter with a great welcome? Certainly! Yet these men also had the free choice to reject the offer, and they did! Those who believe in predestination would say that God decided from the beginning that they were going to hell anyway. This perspective would force us to look at the invitation in this parable as anything but authentic! Calvinists cast a strange light on the very character of God, who, in their estimation, invites people to Himself, having already determined that they cannot come!

But God truly has a glorious purpose and plan for each person who has ever lived. Some, though, reject it, for each of us has a free choice. Luke 7:30 (NASB) says, "But the Pharisees and the lawyers rejected God's purpose for themselves, not having been baptized by John."

Now if this verse is true, then no one could say that God, from the beginning of time, predestined these men to eternal damnation, and yet at the same time say that God had prepared an honorable purpose for them. God's purpose (God's will) for the Pharisees is clearly stated in this passage. His purpose for them was to heed John's message (repent) and to be baptized by him. Yet, they rejected God's purpose. Consequently, even though the Pharisees (in general) were lost and did not enter the kingdom of God (Matthew 5:20), it is declared by Luke 7:30 that God did not predestine them to this end! For God's plan for them was very clearly that they repent, be baptized, and actually enter the kingdom of God!

Therefore, we are indeed held accountable for our response to God's plan for our lives (and that plan is a blessed one). God has a plan for you, my friend. Don't reject it!

The Scriptures simply do not teach that people missed heaven because they were not elected from the beginning of time. But they very emphatically say that people missed the kingdom because they were disobedient, rejected Christ, disbelieved, had no faith, etc. Notice the countless passages in the Old Testament where God is calling *His people* to get right and return. How utterly impractical if they could not respond to His call because they were not predestined to heaven (not "enabled" to respond)!

Look at the many passages where God says He will bless people if they turn away from their sin. The entirety of the Word of God is the Good News of God's grace, not a rigged story. It is a calling of God that holds in question the rebellion of man. God would have never questioned their rebellion if they were simply doing what He predestined them to do (if they had no choice in the matter).

In reference to all the imperatives of Scripture, Calvinism would say that we can try to "repent," "strive," "enter," "believe," "trust," "obey," "ask," and "seek" all we want, but if we are not predestined, we just have to accept the fact that God was "pleased" to foreordain us to hell.

Please take the time to read just some of the passages that refer to God's call to get right with Him, and realize that He would have never made these calls, without giving the ability and grace to respond: Isaiah 1:18–20; 55:1–3, 6; 59:1–2; Jeremiah 3:12–13; 4:14; 7:5–7; 18:11; Ezekiel 18:30–32; 33:11; Hosea 12:6; 14:1; Jonah 3:10; Zephaniah 2:3; Zechariah 1:3; 7:12–14; Malachi 3:7.

We are held accountable for choosing to respond to these admonitions. Notice, also, God's declaration of the choice of man: Isaiah 65:12, 66:4; 2 Chronicles 36:15–16; Proverbs 1:24; Jeremiah 17:13; Joshua 24:15.

What a joy it is to know that we all have the opportunity to respond to the Greatest Commandment ever given, "You shall love the Lord your God with all your heart and with all your soul and with all your mind" (Matthew 22:37 – ESV).

All these commands, admonitions, calls and warnings, though given to all the Israelites, were rejected by many. They also have been given to all the world, yet have been rejected by many. In other words, if God has predestined certain men to hell, why would He at the same time include these in His command to walk in His ways, and hold them accountable for such? It would be impossible for them to obey Him! Accountability would, therefore, be nullified. But the truth is, God voices His calls and commands to all men, and each person has been given the free choice (and responsibility) to respond. Those who choose to receive His call with joy, commitment, and obedience, find great fulfillment and peace, having accepted by faith God's purpose for their lives.

In Matthew 21:28–32, we find Jesus telling us a parable of two sons, one who gives lip service, yet is disobedient, and another who says, "no" first, but then chooses to repent and be obedient. Jesus asks the question, "Which of the two did the will of his father?" (Matthew 21:31 – ESV). Notice, the father (representing God, of course) has one general will for both sons in this passage, that being to do work in his vineyard. Whereas God's will differs in specific note with each one of us, His general will for all of us is that of working in His field, His kingdom. The implication of the passage is that even though one of the sons did not do his father's will, that *will* was indeed *to work in the vineyard*. In other words, the father did not purpose for that son to miss out on life through arbitrary predeterminations, for his purpose (will) for both sons was that each have part in his father's life and work!

The tax-gatherers and harlots, even though they chose to rebel against God initially, repented and were obedient. In other words, God does not have one *good* will for those who get saved and another *condemned* will for those who never do. His will for all is that they serve Him! The religious leaders as a whole, even though they gave lip service to God, were disobedient. Then, even more contrary to God's desire, they did not even change their minds (v. 32) having seen the positive response made by these wicked people who heard the preaching of John. Why would Jesus have expected them to change their minds if He had from the beginning of time determined that they could not do such? But His will for them was that they see the response of the tax-gatherers and harlots, be convicted, and believe. Why didn't they? They chose to reject Christ! These so-called leaders will not enter the Kingdom of God (Matthew 5:20), not because God predestined them to hell, for according to this passage, God's will was for them to repent and to serve in the Kingdom of God. They will not enter the kingdom because they chose not to believe and obey!

God is not playing toy soldiers! You do have a free will! You must make a choice! Repent! Believe! Obey! Follow! *Live!*

Isaiah says, "In repentance and rest you shall be saved, in quietness and trust is your strength. But you were not willing" (30:15 – NASB). This passage declares that salvation comes when we repent and trust ("rest"). The only reason some are condemned is because they are "not willing."

Speaking of God's rain for the harvest, Jeremiah proclaimed, "Your iniquities have turned these away, and your sins have withheld good from you" (Jeremiah 5:25 – NASB). If this verse is true, then "good" would have come their way if they had *chosen* to "fear" God (v. 22). This brings us to our next chapter concerning the results of rejecting God's salvation. *Warning*! The results are eternally severe!

CHAPTER 8

I LOVE YOU! DON'T WAIT UNTIL IT'S TOO LATE!

"For many are called, but few are chosen" (Matthew 22:14 – ESV).

Why are only a few chosen? Is it because God does not desire all men to be saved? No (see chapter 4 of this book)! Is it because salvation is not for everybody? No (see chapter 2)! Is it because Jesus did not really die for all people? No (see chapter 5)! Is it because God does not invite each person to salvation? No (see chapter 3)! Is it because we don't have any choice in the matter? No (see chapter 7)!

Only a few are chosen because only a few people actually respond with their free choice to accept by faith the invitation to salvation that God offers to all men.

The above passage is the conclusion to the parable of the marriage feast found in Matthew 22:1–14. The *many called* are the masses who are offered God's salvation. Many of these reject His invitation. The *few chosen* are those who accept the invitation to come and receive salvation based on God's grace, not on their own goodness. The man who was cast out "into the outer darkness" (vss. 11–13) was called, and he came. But he was not chosen because he came on his own authority, by his own merit and/or goodness ("no wedding garment"). The only way that you and I are accepted (chosen) into God's kingdom is through wearing the robes of righteousness that come from Christ. The only way we can receive this "wedding garment" is by having a personal relationship with Jesus who gives us *His* righteousness. We must have faith in the grace of God who "made Him who knew no sin to be sin on our behalf, that we might become the righteousness of God in Him" (2 Corinthians 5:21 – NASB). See also Romans 5:1; 8:3–4 and Philippians 3:9.

The consequences of not responding to Christ are quite severe (Matthew 22:7, 13).

Christ shares in Luke 19 a parable concerning stewardship. Having given ten slaves money with which to do business, the nobleman went on a journey. Those who chose to be faithful slaves, having faith that their master would hold them accountable and provide for them if they were faithful, were rewarded greatly. Anyone who chose to reject the command of his master and not handle "business" was put to shame. We also see in this parable a group of citizens who did not want the nobleman as their master. They were even adamant about it (v. 14). These were killed for their rebellion. Why were they held accountable to that extent if God had predestined them to rebel? But He did not predetermine such! They *chose* to rebel all on their own and paid dearly for it!

"So I will choose their delusions, and bring their fears on them; because, when I called, no one answered, when I spoke they did not hear; but they did evil before My eyes, and *chose* that in which I do not delight" (Isaiah 66:4 – NKJV).

The Scriptures are filled with passages holding man accountable for his response to God. "For we must all appear before the judgment seat of Christ, that each one may be recompensed for his deeds in the body, according to what he has done, whether good or bad" (2 Corinthians 5:10 – NASB). We have either chosen the "good" path in life, or the "bad," the right or the wrong, the righteous or the ungodly. There are two paths in life, not many, and not a gray area in the middle. The Bible always speaks of two, and describes the consequences of choosing not to exercise faith in Christ Jesus!

Why did God "give over" the wicked (Romans 1:24–26)? Was it because they had not been predestined to heaven? No! Verses 20–21 state that they were without excuse because God had made Himself known to them, but they did not honor Him. Why would God have expected these lost people to honor Him, if they could not have possibly done so on their own?

Why are the unfruitful cast into the fire (Luke 3:9)? Because they were not predestined to eternal life? No! It was because they did not bear good fruit! Luke 3:8 states that true repentance leads to fruit bearing. Why do some reap eternal life while others reap wrath and indignation (Romans 2:7–8)? These verses make it clear that their reward is directly related to their response to the kindness of God (Romans 2:4–5), whether that response be repentance, or stubbornness and disobedience.

Why did God remove the hedge around Judah, His vineyard, so that it would be consumed (Isaiah 5)? Because, after all that God had done to provide a "fertile hill" with a "choice vine," Judah only increased in their sin and rebellion. God even said, "What more was there to do for my vineyard, that I have not done in it?" (Isaiah 5:4 – ESV). Well, He could have simply predestined them to respond positively, and they would have produced (become) good grapes. But again, this is not the way or the will of God. He *had* done all He could. They simply rebelled by an act of their own free will.

Speaking of Jerusalem, Jeremiah says, "And many nations will pass by this city; and they will say to one another, 'Why has the LORD done thus to this great city?'" The answer is not, "Well, He predestined them to this destruction." The biblical answer is, "Because they forsook the covenant of the LORD their God and bowed down to other gods and served them" (Jeremiah 22:8–9 – NASB).

Jesus said, "Enter by the narrow gate;... For the gate is narrow and the way is hard, that leads to life, and those who find it are few" (Matthew 7:13–14 – RSV). Why do only a few find life, just as only a few are chosen? Because few are actually willing to do what Jesus says to do (Matthew 7:24–27). They are unwilling to follow Him as Lord and Master! We must choose to do God's will if we expect to enter the Kingdom of God (Matthew 7:21–23). We cannot do this on our own power, but as we make ourselves available to the Holy Spirit in faith, we can!

How can I be sure to enter? How can I be sure to know Him and be one of His disciples? Abide in His Word by doing what He says to do (Matthew 7:24–25 and John 8:31–32) and you will not reap the consequences of those who choose to ignore and disobey His Word (Matthew 7:26–27).

If you want to enter the kingdom, just ask. Luke 11:13 (NASB) says, "If you then, being evil, know how to give good gifts to your children, how much more shall your heavenly Father give the Holy Spirit to those who *ask* Him?" Here the Bible says that God will give you His very own Spirit if you ask Him! But we must ask in faith as James 1:5–7 states. God encourages us to ask for wisdom, but if we ask without faith, we cannot expect to receive anything from the Lord.

Remember the woman at the well? Jesus said to her, "If you knew the gift of God, and who it is that is saying to you, 'Give me a drink,' you would have asked him, and he would have given you living water" (John 4:10 – ESV). If you want real life in Christ, the Bible says to *ask*! For those who would say that Jesus said this to that particular woman because He knew she was one of the elect, let me say two things.

First of all, Jesus invited many to Himself who rejected Him. In other words, Jesus didn't just offer salvation to those who would receive it because they had been predestined. Secondly, the very nature of this story was to illustrate the truth that God loves each individual, for this woman was a Samaritan, the kind of person that the Jews hated with a great racial passion. Her immorality was such that the people of her own town would have listed her with the wicked and the condemned. The disciples were surprised to see Jesus even talking to her (John 4:9 and 27). In other words, the very essence of this passage demonstrated that Christ came to save *all* peoples and not just the Jews or any other special group. After all Christ did to break down racial, social, gender, and religious barriers, to say that this woman just happened to be one of the elect that God had predestined, is to miss the very point of the passage!

If you want the blessings of Christ, just ask in faith! God has prepared before all time your access into the kingdom, and that is through faith in the grace of God (a trusting response to Christ's atonement).

"The one who conquers will be clothed thus in white garments, and I will never blot his name out of the book of life..." (Revelation 3:5 – ESV). In other words, God will blot out the names of some, that being those who do not respond to His call. We certainly do not believe that anyone can lose their salvation, once they are born of God. Therefore, this passage must reveal the eternal providence of all names in that glorious book, unless they are removed because of unbelief. In other words, God would not have had their names there to begin with if He had already predestined them to hell (nor would He have mentioned any potential of them being erased if He Himself had already predestined them to heaven). This "unbelief" is the same reason given in other passages for those who are cut off (Romans 11:20 and Hebrews 3:19).

Speaking of the enemies of God (Psalm 69:18), Psalm 69:28 (ESV) says, "Let them be blotted out of the book of the living; let them not be enrolled among the righteous." God has provided for your name to be in the book of life, but you must respond in faith to the Lamb of God, Jesus Christ. He shed His blood for your sins and mine on a cross at a place called Calvary, so that we might be saved from damnation.

Spend time reading a host of other passages that reveal the truth that God really does hold us accountable for our response to His Word and call. Some more in the gospels are: Matthew 3:10; 10:32–33; 10:37–39; 11:20–24; 13:1–9, 18–23; 16:24–27; 18:21–35; 22:4–7; 24:45–51; 25:1–13, 14–30, 31–46; Luke 6:35-38; 10:25–37; 11:31–32; 12:31–34; 14:16–24; John 3:18, 36; 6:53–58; and one among so many in the Old Testament (besides all those listed in chapter 7 of this book) is Deuteronomy 28:1–68.

The host of passages like Isaiah 1:18–20, make the call of God very clear. You will reap according to that way in which you respond. "If you consent and obey, you will eat the best of the land, but if you refuse and rebel, you will be devoured by the sword. Truly, the mouth of the Lord has spoken" (Isaiah 1:19–20 – NASB). Those who would share a different theology would negate that which "the Lord has spoken." Why bother with all these warnings (too numerous to count throughout all of God's Word), if you can't really respond to them anyway?

Also, passages like Jeremiah 4:18 (NASB) show the reason judgment came: "Your ways and your deeds have brought these things to you. This is your evil. How bitter!" Also, "Have you not done this to yourself, by your forsaking the LORD your God?" (Jeremiah 2:17 – NASB). Also, "I am bringing disaster on this people, the fruit of their plans, because they have not listened to My words, and as for My law, they have rejected it also" (Jeremiah 6:19 – NASB).

The Scriptures are very clear. There is a severe judgment upon those who choose to reject God's calls, invitations, admonitions, commands, grace, etc.! That judgment comes, not because of the foreordination of God, but because of man's refusal to exercise his free will in repentance and faith.

Ezekiel 18:1–32 shows that you do indeed reap what you sow. You are judged based upon the kind of life you choose, whether or not you turn to do right in God's eyes. Each of us must do so by trusting in Christ's power, not our own. But, indeed, *turn* is what we must do in response to God's Word.

Other passages which speak of the consequences of our rejecting God's Word are: Romans 2:3–11; Proverbs 1:23–33; Nehemiah 9:30; and 1 Corinthians 10:1–12.

Why speak of the conviction of Holy Spirit as found in John 16, if God's grace is irresistible, if it forces you to respond? Conviction is made obsolete. Repentance is made obsolete. Faith is made obsolete. All these terms melt into meaningless vocabulary in the preprogramming of God in Calvinism.

Read Hebrews 3:12–19. Why "take care" and why encourage one another unless we really do have an opportunity to have an impact (a choice) on our own destiny? How could God be provoked (v. 17), if He preprogrammed them to respond in this way. He would simply be pleased, as the Calvinist says, to see them doing what He predestined them to do. But the Bible says God *was* "provoked" when Israel, after being delivered from bondage in Egypt, would not believe and obey Him. If God had predestined them to be disbelieving and disobedient, He certainly would not be provoked by their behavior, for such behavior would simply be the result of His own doing. Yet, He *is* provoked when we do not believe and obey, because He has given us the free will to respond. After all He has done for us in Christ, especially *the cross*, certainly God is angry when we do not respond positively!

The positive side of this chapter, which speaks of the severe consequences of rejecting Christ, is that these passages support the truth that *you do have a choice* in this matter of salvation.

Now, upon having heard this truth, read Hebrews 10:26–39! How is it possible to "insult the Spirit of grace" (v. 29 – NASB), if that grace is irresistible? If God's grace is irresistible (as taught in Calvinism), then it would be impossible for one to insult the Spirit of Grace, for the only possible response to God's grace would be a positive one, if indeed it is irresistible.

One may ask, "What about those He predestined to hell? Can they not insult Him?" Well, first of all, if a person is predestined to hell, they could not insult His grace, for God (according to Calvinism) does not even offer His grace to that person. Therefore, there would be no opportunity for Him to be insulted. Secondly, how could God possibly be insulted at that which He Himself predestined?

2 Corinthians 6:1 (NASB) says, "And working together with Him, we also urge you not to receive the grace of God in vain." This verse would not be in the Bible if it were not actually possible to receive God's grace in vain. Again, if God's grace is irresistible, how could it be received in vain? That would be an impossibility! But the truth is a person can resist God's grace! A person can insult His Spirit! For in the sacrifice of His own Son, God's grace has been offered to all. Certainly, those who reject such grace insult Him entirely!

"You men who are stiff-necked and uncircumcised in heart and ears are always resisting the Holy Spirit; you are doing just as your fathers did" (Acts 7:51 – NASB). When Stephen gave his defense, he concluded with the condemnation that those present Jews (as a whole) did exactly what their forefathers had done. They rebelled against ("resisted") the work of the Holy Spirit. They murdered Christ (Acts 7:52)! Regardless of Calvinist claims, the Bible says that the Holy Spirit was *resisted* by many!

After all God had promised to do for His people He said, "Moreover all these curses shall come upon you…because you did not serve the LORD your God with joy and gladness of heart, for the abundance of everything" (Deuteronomy 28:45–47 – NKJV).

Indeed, the consequences of rejecting God's grace are enormous. We must respond in faith to what God reveals to us in Christ Jesus. And we must respond before it's too late! For "the day of the Lord will come like a thief in the night" (1 Thessalonians 5:2 – ESV).

"Seek the LORD while He may be found; Call upon Him while He is near. Let the wicked forsake his way, and the unrighteous man his thoughts; and let him return to the LORD, and He will have compassion on him; and to our God, for He will abundantly pardon" (Isaiah 55:6–7 – NASB).

The scriptural concepts and calls to respond to Christ *before it is too late* are made null and void in Calvinism. For those predestined to heaven cannot possibly miss their divine appointment. And certainly the warning to the rest is useless since they could never respond anyway (as is proclaimed in Calvinism). Yet who are the "wicked" and the "unrighteous" in Isaiah 55:7? Every single person without Christ! These are promised that if they return to God, they will find "compassion" and "pardon." This promise of salvation is offered to all lost or "wicked" people. They simply must repent and turn to God. Be certain that God could not make this promise to all people, if He Himself had already predetermined that He could not keep it!

Jesus says, "For whoever wishes to save his life shall lose it; but whoever loses his life for My sake and the gospel's shall save it" (Mark 8:35 – NASB). Therefore, let me encourage you to lose your life for the sake of Christ and His gospel. Jesus says that in doing so, you will save your life. In the next verse, Jesus goes on to say, "For what does it profit a man to gain the whole world, and forfeit his soul?" (Mark 8:36 – NASB). The only way it is possible for us to forfeit something, is if we have control (ownership) of it to begin with. The Bible says that you will forfeit (lose) your own soul if you do not choose to respond in faith to the call of Jesus Christ.

Aren't you glad we have God's Word to live by, rather than man's words and wisdom? As the Holy Spirit illuminates His Word to us, we can come to know this wonderful God who loves us beyond our imagination!

This brings us to chapter 9 which warns us of the theology of some who would say, "God does not really love each individual (and one of those individuals may be you)!"

CHAPTER 9

I Love You, Contrary to the Opinion of Some!

"And we have come to know and have believed the love which God has for us. God is love, and the one who abides in love abides in God, and God abides in him" (1 John 4:16 – NASB).

Let's ask the question again! "Does God really love me (whoever *me* is)?" Now let's be honest. Does God really love *everybody*? Not in the concept of predestination! If God's choice and love for me has absolutely nothing to do with any merit of my own (and we all believe this is true), and if God chose to die for and save me (an awesome act of love), and yet He chose before all time to send some to hell with no chance for salvation (which Calvinists believe), then God is not love!

Now, He may be love for you, for me, or for someone else, but God is not love for all (that is, as we are saying, if He did not really die for all). For how could God love me if He predestined me to hell? If God, from the beginning of time, decided that I would have no chance for salvation, He certainly does not love me with that sacrificial *agape* love. Calvary, in such a case, was not for me! Therefore, according to Calvinism, whereas God does love some, His essence is not love! Yet the Bible declares that *God is love, and that Christ died for all!*

I say, therefore, if God is love, then He is love to *all* men, seeing that not one person has the merit to deserve love. If God gives only some the ability to exercise faith, and not others, if He only predestines certain people for salvation and deliberately excludes others, then how can anyone say that God is impartial and loves everybody? He couldn't love everybody, and force some to be damned at the same time. But the Calvinist doctrine states that this is exactly what God did in His sovereign will. Well, if that's what He did, then He certainly does not love everybody. But praise God we are not limited to listening to the wisdom of Calvinists, for we have God's own Word which tells us that He does love everybody, that's why He died for all.

It cannot be both ways! Either Jesus did love and die for all, or He predestined some to heaven and some to hell, with no regard to any man's response. Again, it can't be both! I choose to listen to the Bible! The Word of God says Jesus died for all, even the likes of me. And it proclaims that I have a choice to respond to that love.

Those who believe in predestination declare that God deliberately excludes some from salvation. Yet those not "quickened" are held responsible for rejecting God. Again, you can't have it both ways. Either God is in control of man's choice, or man is in control of man's choice. Which will it be? It cannot possibly be both! If God predestines a man to hell (or does not "enable" the man to have faith), then that man can not be "responsible" for rejecting Jesus Christ, when he could not possibly choose to receive or trust Him. That would nullify one being responsible (see "primary cause" in the definition of *responsible*). Again, let's choose the proclamation of the

Scriptures! They proclaim that we have a choice and, therefore, are responsible (see again chapter 7 of this book).

That would be like your being my boss and saying, "You bring the electric tools and I'll provide the electricity." Yet, you do not bring the generator, but you still hold me accountable because my tools don't work. Would that be right? Certainly not!

Calvinism says that God is sovereign over man's choice, yet holds him accountable for it, when God had already *fixed it* where some men could not believe. Calvinists use and affirm the phrase "man's responsibility" because there is no way around this scriptural concept. It is found from one end of the Bible to the other. But the Calvinist doctrine never implies that a man not predestined to heaven could actually choose by an act of his will to trust Jesus. Calvinism verbalizes that both the lost man and the regenerated man make a choice, but they do not mean that either one of them could actually have chosen either of two options. Calvinism believes that the choice one makes is simply whatever God did or did not enable him to do. For instance, in Calvinism, the saved man could not have actually chosen to reject God's salvation ("irresistible grace"). Nor could the lost man have actually chosen to exercise faith in Christ ("total depravity"). Therefore, the Calvinist's use of the words "man's responsibility" and "choice" is falsehood (in that the vocabulary is an attempt to line up with God's Word, while the doctrine actually denies it).

What if a father said to his son, "John, take the car, go to the store, and buy some milk and bread." Yet, the father will not give John the keys to the car (and just as we cannot reach salvation on our own works, the store is by far too great a distance to reach by walking). Later, the father says, "John, why did you not get the milk and bread?" John says, "You would not give me the keys to the car." The father says, "That's no excuse! You are punished!" Would this be right? Of course, not! Yet this is the character Calvinists cast upon our great God and Savior! They say that the Heavenly Father deliberately withholds the "keys" to salvation from some men, yet holds them accountable for rejecting His salvation, a redemption that was never offered.

What if you have two children and one has been "chosen" and the other not? Does this describe the loving God of the Bible? Does this truly represent the teachings of Scripture in regard to the character of God?

Love and Faith, two powerful scriptural themes, are totally negated in predestination. The Bible is filled with passages calling and commanding me to have faith in and to love God. But if God forces me to respond to Him with some sovereign act of power, then my response to Him could never be considered faithful love, as the Bible defines it (the "cheerful" response of a devoted heart). It would only be an overpowering move of God.

The great tendency through the ages of many theologians and religious leaders has been to develop a belief that *they* are the only chosen ones! We must let the Scriptures warn us of those who would mislead us: "They eagerly seek you, not commendably, but they wish to shut you out, in order that you may seek them" (Galatians 4:17 – NASB). There are many religions and denominations that make you think *they* are the only ones, hoping you will seek to join their kind of thinking, as did the Jews referenced here in Paul's warning to the Galatians. Romans 11:32 (NASB) says, "But God has shut up all in disobedience, that He might show mercy to all."

How heart breaking it must be to go through life wondering if God really loves you. There is no scriptural reason for this. God's love is not limited to a few. It is offered to all! We simply must receive it in faith.

Calvinists would even have us believe that those who did not make it into the Promised Land had already been predestined to hell by God (that some of God's own "chosen people" had already been foreordained to hell before He chose them to be His people). Yet the

Bible says, "the Lord, having first of all saved a people out of Egypt, later destroyed those *who did not believe*" (Jude 5 – HCSB). This matches the reference in Hebrews 3:12–19, in relation to the reason they were not able to enter ("because of unbelief").

Am I not to love like God loves? The biblical answer is emphatically, "Yes!" God said, "Love your neighbor as yourself!" (Leviticus 19:18; Matthew 22:39). "Love your enemies, and do good, and lend, expecting nothing in return; and your reward will be great, and *you will be sons of the Most High*; for He Himself is kind to ungrateful and evil men" (Luke 6:35 – NASB). Also, The LORD is... kind in all his works (Psalm 145:17 – ESV). This is the God of the Bible! Let us not craft our own!

Therefore, the word to God's children is, "Love the sojourner therefore; for you were sojourners in the land of Egypt" (Deuteronomy 10:19 – RSV).

We are to be like the Father. What is the Father like? *He loves everybody*! Are you sure? Who is "my neighbor"? Do you remember the story of the Good Samaritan? This is who God loves! Who is that? Everybody and anybody who needs love. Are we to love others more than God does? Certainly not! He is our Example! Do not allow anyone to mislead you to destroy the vast amounts of the Word of God that proclaim His love for you and for me and for every single person!

The Bible *never* says anything like, "God was pleased to foreordain some men to hell." Yet this is the definite teaching of predestination. When you apply the doctrinal statements of Calvinism, you find them undermining the Word of God from one end of the Bible to the other. The dynamic relationship God desires to have with His children is all but negated. The relationship is diminished to that of an inventor toying with his invention.

This leads us to our final chapter. God has given us His word that He loves us, and wants to have a genuine relationship with us. Believe God, for every word of God is pure (Psalm 12:6; 19:8)!

CHAPTER 10

I LOVE YOU! I HAVE GIVEN YOU MY WORD!

"From childhood you have known the sacred writings which are able to give you the wisdom that leads to salvation through faith which is in Christ Jesus" (2 Timothy 3:15 – NASB).

If "every word of God is pure" (Proverbs 30:5 – KJV) and "God cannot lie" (Titus 1:2 – KJV), then you can know beyond any shadow of a doubt that God loves you, for He has indeed given us His word. According to the passage above, "the sacred writings," that which we call the Word of God, are able to give people the wisdom that leads to salvation through faith. If God predestined us to heaven or hell, the Scriptures then could do no such thing. But because God does love you and me and everybody, His Word can be trusted and followed by anyone and everyone.

It is certain that what God decides to do, the direction He moves, the power He allows, the powers He removes... no one can thwart His control. But be not deceived, the Scriptures themselves make it very clear that one decision God has made, which is foundational in the gospel, is that every man has a choice to accept, follow, serve, obey, honor and know Him... or ...reject, rebel, mock, disobey, despise and ignore Him. No one will ever thwart this decision of God's either! Just because God (who is indeed omniscient) already knows what a man will choose, the integrity of that choice is not violated. Otherwise, it is a waste of time to encourage others to know God. For if, through predestination, God has not made the opportunity for you to know Him, you can search, spend time and energy, long for, and seek to know Him, but it will all be in vain.

But praise God the Scriptures say, "For I know the plans that I have for you, declares the LORD, plans for welfare and not for calamity to give you a future and a hope. Then you will call upon Me and come and pray to Me, and I will listen to you. And you will seek Me and find Me, when you search for Me with all your heart" (Jeremiah 29:11–13 – NASB).

I plead with you, "Listen to the voice of Christ!" He loves you. He has given you His word. His actions have more than backed up that word. And the Scriptures repeat the spirit of and the recording of His love over and over and over. Surely, you would prefer to listen to the words of Christ rather than that of any man (even Calvin, Edwards, Spurgeon, etc.). Certainly, historically, Calvin's work in the reformation led to some great moves away from Catholicism, but does that mean that our Bible becomes that which he conceived? Certainly not! Calvin's concept of total depravity went so far to the other extreme that it depicts man as totally incapable of responding to the grace and call of God. This is contrary to the Word of God. Calvin needed to ease back enough to realize that whereas God indeed provided everything necessary for salvation, man is required to respond with his God-given free will. Certainly, there is no person who could ever earn, deserve, merit, or work for this salvation. It is a gift from God! But God's own scriptural demand is that man respond in faith and obedience, and this is to be of his own volition.

Let's all vote to set aside the glorifying of man's words, and uphold the words of Christ, which are all too often complicated by new words and concepts with new definitions and systems of theology that simply confuse (or completely deny) the truth of Scripture.

Calvinism portrays a love that is limited ("limited atonement")! In this doctrine, whatever reason it is that God used to predestine men, we know that reason could *not* have one single thing to do with us in and of ourselves. Otherwise, God would be a respecter of persons, showing partiality, which the Bible denies! Therefore, whatever the sovereign reason God used to save some of us and damn the others, forces the question as to how such love could be trusted. For how could one assume and know that he was included in that choice? One's faith in such a case, rather than resting in the true love of Calvary's Lamb (the Christ of the cross), may only be a meager hope that God had chosen him over against someone else.

But in the cross I can boast, for in Christ's love at Calvary, even I am included, for all were there included! You can trust that He included you, too!

If Jesus ever became angry, I suppose we would think of the time He "cleansed" the temple (when He cast out all those buying and selling). What do you suppose ignited that anger? They were taking the court of the Gentiles, that place where *any man in this world* could come, inquire, worship, and know the God of this universe, and they were destroying its God-given purpose (to be a house of prayer for all peoples). Jesus came "to seek and to save that which was lost" (Luke 19:10 – KJV). All who have ever lived fit into this category.

If Jesus became angry enough to make "a whip of cords" (John 2:15 – NKJV) and drive the merchants out with great force, and keep them out (as Mark tells us), then it is certain that God is serious about the Gospel being for everybody, and that *not just some are invited* and called to salvation. Therefore, *you are loved*! And my prayer for you is that you respond to that love in faith, believing that Christ Jesus died for you, too. You may ask, "What do I do?"

Ask! Let me refer you to Luke 11:13; James 1:5–7; John 4:10–14; and Matthew 7:7–8.

Ask *today*!

"If you seek Him, He will let you find Him" (2 Chronicles 15:2b – NASB).

Seek *today*!

"Repent and be baptized every one of you in the name of Jesus Christ for the forgiveness of your sins" (Acts 2:38 – ESV).

Repent and be baptized *today*!

"If you confess with your mouth that Jesus is Lord and believe in your heart that God raised him from the dead, you will be saved" (Romans 10:9 – ESV).

Confess and believe *today*!

"For whosoever shall call upon the name of the Lord shall be saved" (Romans 10:13 – KJV).

Call on Him *today*!

Conclusion

As I said in the beginning, I certainly do believe that God has foreordained or *predestined* some things, since the Bible uses the term. I simply believe that He predetermined certain aspects of our lives, as declared in Scriptures, not that He predestined some to heaven and others to hell.

Also, may I say, it is a soul searching venture to make declarations about God, knowing that the last desire of our heart is to misrepresent Him in any way. The Lord knows I have wrestled over and over with the precise wording of this book, knowing that our knowledge of Him is not complete. For this reason I have tried simply to express what the Bible actually *says*, and not attempt to develop a concept of the nature of God that is conceived in the mind and logic of a man.

A Foundation for Truth: The Bible, God's Word

Please recognize this: We have one written authority, and that is the Word of God! "But know this first of all, that no prophecy of Scripture is a matter of one's own interpretation, for no prophecy was ever made by an act of human will, but men moved by the Holy Spirit spoke from God" (2 Peter 1:20–21). Also, see 2 Timothy 3:16.

If we believe that some man's interpretation of the Bible is our authority, then we have no common ground upon which to seek the truth. So, be honest with yourself and ask, "Is my authority the Bible (what it *says*)?" Or did I derive my belief from logical human deductions from thoughts concerning something found in the Bible?

If "every word of God is pure" (Proverbs 30:5) and "God cannot lie" (Titus 1:2), then we can assume that God will not contradict Himself in His Word. So, when we have passages that *seem* to contradict each other, we must assume that we have not appropriately interpreted at least one of them. And certainly, if our interpretation of one forces us to discount or negate a whole host of other passages, then we must question our interpretation.

We cannot convince one another that our *interpretation* of the Scriptures defines truth. For if our foundation for truth is not what the Bible *says*, but is what certain men say the Bible *means*, then our foundation for truth is quickly reduced to any person's own development of their own logic. Let's stick with the Scriptures! Certainly, each of us will settle on particular explanations of passages, but if our conclusions cannot be reflected elsewhere in what the Bible says, then how shall we be convinced we have arrived at truth?

In the same way that I have not given a complete exegesis of all the passages used in this book, I also shall not attempt a detailed exegesis of all the passages used to support the Calvinist doctrine. I would, however, like to pinpoint a few passages, so that you will have some idea how I understand them. But before I do that, let me just mention that whatever you do with these apparent difficult passages, don't let a potential misinterpretation destroy (or completely negate) the host of clearly understandable Scriptures we have already covered in this book. Unless otherwise noted, all Scriptures quoted in this "Conclusion" are from the NASB (not *updated* version).

Remember "Foreknowledge" in the Predeterminations of God's Choice
(Romans 8, Ephesians 1, etc.)

To begin with, let me direct you to Romans 8:29–30. This passage is very straight forward. God "foreknew" those who would respond to Him in faith, for God is omniscient, as we know. "Whom He foreknew, He also predestined." It does not say, "God predestined some to become known by Him and others not!" What it does specifically say is that God, in His sovereign will, decided (predestined) that true believers would become conformed to the image of Christ. What God predestined was not the eternal destiny of each man, but that those who would exercise faith in Jesus would actually become like Him. So praise God that when we are saved, we are not just given a ticket to heaven, but God actually does something wonderful with the likes of us, and conforms us to the image of His Son! And He does that with every single believer, for He predestined it to be so.

So, please keep this scriptural truth (principle) in mind as you read through other passages that utilize the words that Calvinists use to support predestination. What does the Bible actually *say*? Does it say that God predestined some to heaven and others to hell? Or does it not simply say that God predestined certain things for the lives of those who are saved, those who choose to respond to Christ in faith?

Having already established the scriptural truth of God's foreknowledge, and having clearly seen the essence of the gospel over and over in detail: the cross, repentance, faith, and the scope of the whole world, we have to be careful that when we see the words *chose* and *predestined* that we do not abandon the text, and insert some Calvinistic preconceived ideas about those terms. For if we do so, we will develop an interpretation that ignores all we have already established.

For instance, Ephesians 1:4 does not *say* that God chose us to go to heaven over against others chosen for hell. But He chose to do something wonderful in the lives of those who are "faithful in Christ Jesus" (v. 1), those who truly hope in Christ (v. 12). He predestined that we would be made into people who are "holy and blameless before Him." Also, in verse 5, He did not predestine us to heaven over against other people who are sent to hell, He simply predetermined that He, "according to the kind intention of His will," would adopt believers as His very own children. Praise God for such a fantastic spiritual blessing (1:3). God could have just predetermined that we who believe in Him would get to be slaves in His kingdom. But in His marvelous grace, He decided before all time that we would be able to cry out, "Abba! Father!" (Romans 8:15). Praise the Heavenly Father, for He has adopted us!

2 Thessalonians 2:13 says, "... because God has chosen you from the beginning for salvation through sanctification by the Spirit and faith in the truth." Notice the sentence or thought does not end with the word *salvation*. In other words, what God chose was not their salvation over against someone else's damnation. For those who were lost are identified in verse 10 as those who "*did not receive* the love of the truth so as to be saved." This implies that they had the opportunity to receive it. If they had received it, they would have been saved! But for others, those whom God foreknew would receive the truth, He chose the method of salvation: "through sanctification by the Spirit and faith in the truth," that same truth those in verse 10 chose to reject (not to receive). In other words, the method of salvation was through one's faith (not through one's works!), and the sanctification process is a work of the Holy Spirit. Our works could never accomplish this! This gives all the credit indeed to Him whom we trust, rather than to man who often trusts in some work he thinks he may accomplish. God does this that we might actually gain His glory (v. 14), for no glory of our own would ever merit salvation.

Notice, again, the Word never says He chose some for hell, for those who are sentenced to hell are not getting what God predestined, but a "retribution" for their lack of knowledge of God, and their unwillingness to "obey the gospel" (2 Thessalonians 1:8).

What about Acts 13:48 where it says, "…and as many as had been *appointed* to eternal life believed"?

Well, let's look at the context. Notice in Acts 13:38 where "forgiveness of sins is proclaimed to you." Who is *you*? To just a certain few, or to *all* who heard the proclamation? Certainly the latter, for God would not be deceitful! And notice in Acts 13:39 the ones who are set free: "everyone who believes"! You could not, in truth, proclaim forgiveness of sins to everyone if God will not allow everyone to be forgiven.

Also, Acts 13:40 exhorts them to "take heed" that judgment may not overcome them. How could they possibly take heed if God had not given them the free choice to repent and believe?

Did God, before the beginning of time, really haphazardly judge (predestine) some as unworthy of eternal life? Well, the truth is, all of us are unworthy in and of ourselves, but what does the Word *say*? Acts 13:46 says that the Jews *repudiated* the word of God, and *judged themselves* "unworthy of eternal life." They were offered the Word, but they rejected it. According to the Scriptures, the Jews were the ones who should have most easily and obviously received it. So their failure to find eternal life was not the predestination of God, but their own rejection of Christ, their own unwillingness to accept the Word.

Now, then, notice Acts 13:48 does not say that God appointed some to hell, and these to heaven. The word here is used in the same sense that God *elected* or *chose* those whom He foreknew would place faith in Him. He appointed them to eternal life whom He foreknew. For those who go to hell, are those who "repudiate" the Word (13:46). They are offered eternal life, but reject it. Those who receive heaven are believers. Forgiveness of sins is proclaimed to them, and they believe (13:38–39). The Lord simply designed that "as many as had been appointed" (these whom He foreknew at Antioch) would come to their moment of salvation simultaneously to show the pouring out of the Holy Spirit on the Gentiles (13:46–47), and for the spreading of the gospel (13:49).

When we have a position to fill or a task to accomplish, we appoint people whom we already know. We don't haphazardly appoint people with whom we have no relation! God appoints people He already knows, those He *foreknows*. So, again, it is the scriptural principle of foreknowledge that is crucial in the interpretation.

Just because God knows what I am going to decide (believe or repudiate), that does not alter my free choice. God's being eternal does not change or violate the fact or act of our free choice in the realm of time.

Another verse using the word *appoint* is John 15:16. Again, here, Christ has simply appointed us, His children, to the kingdom work of fruit bearing, and has given us access to the Father who will give us the necessary resources to accomplish this commission.

Romans 9-11

Even though I have already commented on some of Romans 9–11, let me attempt to address some misconceptions.

Romans 9:13 says, "Jacob I loved, but Esau I hated." If you pull this verse out of the context of its chapter, and out of the context of the Bible, you may conclude that God simply chooses to love some, hate others, and that's all there is to it. But let's invest a little more effort than that in our pursuit of truth.

First of all, consider the word *hate* in two other passages. Luke 14:26 says, "If anyone comes to Me, and does not *hate* his own father and mother and wife and children and *brothers* and sisters, yes, and even his own life, *he cannot be My disciple.*" 1 John 3:15 says, "Everyone who *hates his brother* is a murderer; and you know that *no murderer has eternal life* abiding in him" (also see: John 13:14–15 and Ephesians 5:25, 28). At face value, one verse says you cannot be a disciple of Jesus unless you hate your brother. The other verse says if you hate your brother you are a murderer who does not have eternal life. Now, we know that disciples do have eternal life (and are not murderers). Therefore, either the Bible contradicts itself, or the word *hate* can and is used differently in these two passages. John develops the understanding that if you have Christ abiding in you, you will show love to the people around you. The Luke passage is about priority in allegiance. It is speaking of the fact that in all your relationships, the one relationship that must take priority is that one you have with God! Your relationship with God should be so far higher in priority that all other relationships look like *hate* in comparison (no close second)!

That is more the essence of the use of the word *hate* we have in Romans 9:13. And you can see this by the context of the chapter, and also, in the context of the verses quoted from the Old Testament. Romans 9:12 is a quote from Genesis 25:23 where the Lord says to Rebecca, "*Two nations are in your womb*; and two peoples will be separated from your body; and one people shall be stronger than the other; *and the older shall serve the younger*." Romans 9:13, therefore, really refers to the nations of Israel (the descendants of Jacob) and Edom (the descendants of Esau). The point of the passage is that in comparison to the *love* shown to Jacob (Israel), His providence for Esau (Edom) looked like *hate*!

You see this truth in the context of Romans 9, looking at the verses immediately preceding this. Read Romans 9:1–8. These Israelites for whom Paul is so concerned are lost. They have, as a whole, rejected their own Messiah. Yet they are the very ones who should have found eternal life in Christ, for theirs was the adoption, the glory, the covenants, the Law, the service, the promises, etc. (v. 4). Indeed they had been blessed (or "loved") far beyond all other nations with these privileges. They had not been chosen to go to heaven instead of other nations, but they were chosen to be the ones to first come to know God, and then to share Him with the nations. God's choosing to love them this way caused His relation to the nation of Edom to look like *hate* in comparison.

Did God fail in His plan (Romans 9:6–8)? Certainly not! For the true children of Israel came through a promise. God promised Abraham he would be a great nation and a blessing to all the families (nations) of the earth (Genesis 12:1–3). Now, when God made this promise, Abraham was old and his wife, Sarah, was barren. God promised that she would bear a son to Abraham. When Romans 9:7 mentions the descendants being named through Isaac, it is for two reasons. One, that man's efforts will never attain this. Therefore, the promise would not come through Ishmael (Abraham and Sarah's effort through Hagar). Second and most crucial, that the promise ultimately spoke of Christ (See Galatians 3:16), who came through Jacob, who had twelve sons, one of whom was Judah, the tribe through which Jesus Christ came.

But without question, the Israelites were blessed ("loved") by God in a very unique way above all other nations, having been given the privilege of being the one nation God chose to bless and foreshadow His own character in how He deals with His true spiritual children in blessings, providence, protection, grace, mercy, love, and salvation. For we see all these blessings from God for Israel in the deliverance from bondage in Egypt, their reception of the Law in the wilderness, the providence of manna, the forgiveness in the bronze serpent, the gift of the promised land, victory over enemies, and on and on. But even though God "loved" Israel in this way more than the "hated" Edomites, that does not mean the Israelites were spiritually saved instead of the Edomites.

Ultimately, it is those who are of Christ who are the true *spiritually saved* children of God (Romans 9:8). For the promise is found in Christ by those who have faith in Him, as did Abraham (Galatians 3:7), not by those who are simply of the blood-line of Abraham, Isaac, and Jacob.

Therefore, Romans 9:13 is not at all about God's predetermining the eternal destiny of the twins, Jacob and Esau, but it is about God's choice concerning through whom the promise of Christ would come (and, again, which nation would experience the physical blessings that foreshadowed God's Fatherhood over His true spiritual children).

Romans 9:15 certainly shows that God can choose whomever He so desires to bless. But if you are inclined to push this verse towards the support of predestination, compare it with the conclusive perspective of Romans 11:32.

In Malachi 1:1–5, not only do we find the origin of Romans 9:13, but we also find God's dealing with Edom in the context such that it confirms that Romans 9:13 is speaking of the nation that came from Esau, and not declaring some arbitrary choice of God to hate a man. Also, Edom's declaration of their own strength to build up their ruins and overcome the "desolation" God had caused, fits Romans 9:16. God indeed is sovereign! Man has no power over His workings, but must cry for God's mercy, mercy that other passages tell us is available through repentance.

For instance, Jeremiah 18 speaks of the sovereignty of God in verses 5–7. Certainly God can, like the potter, declare destruction to any nation He so desires. But His promise is, "If that nation against which I have spoken turns from its evil, *I will* relent concerning the calamity I planned to bring on it" (Jeremiah 18:8). If God had predestined them to destruction, He could not have at the same time made this promise, for their doom would be settled such that nothing could thwart the pending penalty of His judgment.

Therefore, with the context properly in place, you can see that Romans 9:13 does not say that God decided Jacob would go to heaven, and Esau to hell. The eternal destiny of the twins is not at all the focus or doctrine of this passage. Paul is trying to get the Jews (the Israelites by birth) to realize how incredibly blessed they are to have been chosen of God to be the nation through which Christ came. He is praying that they will begin pursuing God by faith, rather than by works.

One may still ask, "Why did God choose the child, Jacob, instead of his twin, Esau?" Well, indeed, God is God. He can do anything He wants to do! Considering His wisdom, ways, and thoughts which are so much higher than any of ours, I'm not sure we are even able to answer this question completely. But we can see what God foreknew about Esau (and possibly, then, why the word *hate* is used, if you are inclined to reject what I just shared above). Read Hebrews 12:15–17.

Even though Esau was sorry that he had lost his birthright ("he sought for it with tears"), he "found no place for repentance." Jesus said, "If you do not repent, you will perish." The Hebrews passage exhorts each of us to, "See to it" that you are not immoral or godless "like Esau." How could we possibly "see to it" if God has already predestined us to "come short of His grace"? But just like Esau made his own choices, the Scriptures are calling us to make better choices than did Esau. God, in His foreknowledge of Esau's choices, used him (accordingly) to fulfill His own purposes.

My purpose in this book was not to spend that kind of time with any one passage, but I thought it necessary to give an example or two of what it takes to untangle misdirected theology that has been developed by pulling passages out of context.

What about Pharaoh? The passage Romans 9:17 quotes is from Exodus. "But, indeed, for this cause I have allowed you to remain, in order to show you My power, and in order to proclaim My name through all the earth" (Exodus 9:16). Pharaoh was already an unbeliever in God. He had chosen his own way. The result of his spiritual stance would be death and separation. As a matter of fact, God had just told him that he would have already been wiped out had God struck him (Exodus 9:15). But God allowed him to "remain" longer in the flesh, so that God might use him to fulfill His purpose of revealing Himself to all mankind ("to proclaim My name through all the earth"). When we talk about God accomplishing His purpose, we must remember that making Himself known to the world is a major part of that purpose, and this is revealed and expressed all through the Scriptures (see verses like Exodus 9:14; 9:16; 9:29; Genesis 12:1–3; Isaiah 45:5–6; Malachi 1:11; John 1:7, 9, 29; Hebrews 1:1–3).

Romans 9:17 reveals to us, that no matter who you are, saved or lost, as we may put it, God has the authority and sovereignty to use you to accomplish His eternal purpose. But when God does use lost or saved people to accomplish His purpose, He does not violate their own free will in responding to Him personally. Pharaoh was a man who had already chosen to dishonor Jehovah (Exodus 9:17). One may rightly ask, "What about Romans 9:18? Does this not prove predestination, or at least that God is controlling man's response?" Don't assume that God just haphazardly decides whom to harden and whom to show mercy. His criterion for such has already been stated in Jeremiah 18.

Also, if you are concerned about who gets to be a vessel for honor (Romans 9:21), then read the promise found in 2 Timothy 2:21. Paul could not declare this truth to Timothy if God's "desire" (Romans 9:18) was haphazardly directed. This was truth Paul expected Timothy to share with all men. Also, when we get to Romans 11, it is very clear that those who find mercy (God's "kindness") and those who find "severity" experience such as a result of their own faith or their own unbelief (Romans 11:22–23), not by some haphazard selection of God.

In other words, God did not predestine Pharaoh to hell so that He could use him in the Exodus story. God "raised" up Pharaoh, a man who was already defying God's glory. God could have simply killed Pharaoh or left him to his own devices, but He used Pharaoh to display His glory. We might also want to inquire as to why God wanted to "show" Pharaoh His "power" (Exodus 9:16). Did God want Pharaoh to know Him? Certainly!

Romans 9:19–20 continues to reveal that God has the sovereignty to use all vessels to His own glory, even those like Pharaoh who are unbelievers. In reading Romans 9:21–23, remember that those who are "prepared for destruction," and those who are "vessels of mercy which He prepared beforehand for glory," are categorized in this way based upon the foreknowledge of God as to who responds in faith (8:29). Also, Romans 11:2 shows God did not reject those "whom He foreknew."

Let me remind you of Paul's heart in Romans 9:1–3, a heart that loves these people more than God does, if predestination to heaven and hell is valid. Also, Paul declares that the Jews "did not *subject themselves* to the righteousness of God" (Romans 10:3). This implies they could have been submissive if they had chosen to do so. Romans 10:11–13 gives an all inclusive truth about this God with whom there is "no distinction." Romans 10:13 has been used to share the gospel all over the world. Such use is a lie if just any person cannot actually call upon the name of the Lord!

Also, Israel's own "transgression" (Romans 11:11) has been used to bring salvation to the Gentiles, "to make them jealous." How could jealously have any impact on what God has already predestined, unless the truth is, they actually do have a choice in the matter? Notice again the words that describe *free will* in verse 15: *rejection* and *acceptance*. And notice again, the words of the will in verses 20 and 23: *unbelief* and *faith*. These words are used here to describe the cause of their being "broken off" or "grafted in."

Notice the overall thrust of Romans 11. This is a description of the Gentiles (wild branches) having access to the kingdom, and Jews (natural branches) who will also be grafted back in if they do not "continue in their unbelief." In other words, those whom Calvinists would say are predestined to go to hell, actually have the ability to repent (discontinue) from their unbelief and be saved. Even the "lost" Jews ("broken off for their unbelief" – 11:20) had the God-given ability to choose to trust God. This is an *all inclusive* gospel call being declared.

Romans 9–11 is an explanation of the eternal purpose of God, not from a perspective of predestination, but to change the perspective of the Jews who thought *they* were the only children of God. The very nature of the message in this section of Scripture is the inclusion of the whole world in the gospel, not the exclusion of certain people as seen in Calvinism. Those who are ultimately excluded are clearly "cut off" for their "unbelief," not because they were prevented by God.

Calvinists will use Romans 9–11 to express a God who limits His love! But the truth declared in this passage is that God, who called and "loved" Israel, will still accomplish His purpose of declaring Himself to all mankind even though they, as a whole, failed to do what they were commissioned to do. God accomplished getting the gospel to the world (the Gentiles), even through the rejection of His own people, even though their acceptance would have shown a more powerful witness (Romans 11:15). Again, God's design for the gospel is an all inclusive scope, seen even in this often misinterpreted section of Scripture. "For God has shut up all in disobedience that He might show mercy to *all*" (Romans 11:32).

Whereas a quick reading of Romans 9–11 may lead one to many questions and misinterpretations, the truth is, these three chapters very specifically declare God's all inclusive gospel and the consequences of man's response.

The Truth

As you encounter the whole counsel of the Word of God, the truth is overwhelming. Remember now, the bulk of passages found all throughout God's Word which we reviewed in the ten chapters of this book. They clearly and repeatedly proclaim these truths:

1. God is love, because that is who He is!

2. God loves you, yes, you, whoever you are! (*whosever*; *any man*; *all*; *the world*, etc.)

3. God's invitation to receive His love is for every single person!

4. God's desire (His will) is for every single person to be saved!

5. Jesus died on the cross to pay the price for the sin of every single person!

6. God has commissioned us to seek to evangelize and disciple every person!

7. God has given each person the free will to choose to accept or to reject His gospel!

8. God has warned man of the consequences of rejecting His invitation!

9. God loves you even though some believe the gospel may not be for *you*!

10. God has given you His word: He loves you! Trust what He *says*!

The Ten Chapters of this book hold a great continuity in sharing a glimpse of the fullness of God's love for all people. You have probably noticed the many ways they are intertwined and overlap at points, but each one reveals a different scriptural perspective on God's love. These truths cause overwhelming question concerning the integrity of the Calvinist doctrine of predestination. Certainly, the entire counsel of the Word of God cannot be seen to support this man-made doctrine!

Please know this, God loves you, whoever you are! Just read His Word, listen to His voice, and respond in faith! As you develop your own concept of truth, please stick with God's Word! Listen precisely to what it *says* and the *way* it says it. Calvinism most definitely has to alter what God's Word says to make it line up with its own belief.

Can you say, "Whosoever shall call upon the name of the Lord shall be saved"?

Can you say, "God desires all men to be saved"?

Can you say, "God loves the whole world" (every individual)?

Can you say, "Jesus died for you" to any person you encounter?

Can you say, "You must make a choice" to any person you encounter?

Can you say, "God calls for every single person to repent, and therefore, gives them the opportunity to do so"?

Can you say, "There are eternal consequences for those who choose to reject Christ"?

Can you say, "God's good news is truly for every single person"?

Can you say, "God loves you, yes, you, whoever you are"?

These are statements overwhelmingly taught in the Word of God!

If you are a Calvinist, will you *be honest* with people and say things like, "God may not really love you, for He did not die for everyone."? ...or... "Commit your life to Christ! But realize this: God may not enable you to have faith. If He doesn't, you are eternally damned."?

Whatever your belief is, be honest! Share the gospel in truth! Are you leaving off what you believe to be true? If you believe in predestination as defined in the introduction of this book, but then you offer the gospel openly to all men, you are a liar! You cannot preach openly to the world, "Jesus died for you. Repent and believe in the gospel," if you believe in predestination. For if you do so, you would be lying! For the way you are offering it, each person is given the impression he or she can respond by choosing either of two options (to accept Christ or to reject Him), when you yourself do not believe they have the free capacity to do such.

Our church sent a team to Africa to share the gospel through drama. The drama focused upon a man whom God created, who was lured away into sin, and who was overcome and placed in bondage to sin. The drama depicts Christ dying for the man, the man being delivered, and great freedom, life, and love resulting. It was quite moving!

If we had been Calvinists and were honest with those in Zambia, we would have been truthful only if we had added at least one more character to the drama: a man who was lovingly created by God, just like the first man, yet not offered the deliverance from sin as the first man was. He would represent those according to Calvinism who have no opportunity for salvation (those who are not chosen, those not predestined to heaven). Is this the message we are called to take to the world? Certainly not!

If a man has ten sons, which ones would he choose to live with him and have an inheritance, and which ones would he choose to send away empty handed? You say, "He provides opportunity for fellowship and fortune for each one. Their future and their experiences unfold as a result of their response to the father's love and providence." You would not say, "He just haphazardly chooses for some to enjoy his wealth and relationship, and chooses banishment for the others." Yet, if you promote predestination, this is exactly how you characterize our Heavenly Father!

May no one assume that in any way I am reducing the grace of God to anything less than our only hope, and joy, and life! Indeed, how eternally gracious He is! But I must declare, according to the Word of God, the call from God over and over is that you and I and every person respond to His Spirit of grace, who indeed is insulted when we reject Him!

The Holy Spirit (including John 6:44)

"Today, if you hear His voice, do not harden your hearts, as when they provoked Me..." (Hebrews 3:7–8). We do "provoke" and insult God's Spirit when we resist His call. The obvious implication here is that if God speaks to us (lets us "hear His voice"), we have the option (choice) to harden our hearts. The implicit command in the verse is to soften our heart (or be sensitive and respond positively to the Holy Spirit). According to Calvinism, if you hear His voice, it would be impossible to harden your heart to this conviction ("voice") of the Holy Spirit ("Irresistible Grace"). But why would God speak to a man, calling him to salvation, and then, yet, not be willing to save him? God would not do such. According to God's Word, we are compelled to hear God's call and respond willingly in faith. Those who rejected his voice perished (Hebrews 3:15–19). But your privilege *now* is, you can choose to soften (not "harden") your heart and rejoice for, "now is the acceptable time, behold, now is the day of salvation" (2 Corinthians 6:2).

"No one can come to Me, unless the Father who sent Me draws him; and I will raise him up on the last day" (John 6:44). Now this verse speaks of the truth that we cannot find God on our own. God must initiate and enable the relationship. In this passage Jesus is trying to get the Jews to let go of their traditions and laws as ways to get to God. They could not get there on their own, as Paul reiterates in Romans 9:31–32, where he says Israel did not "arrive" because they were trying to get there "by works."

Now some people say that John 6:44 reveals that God only draws or grants the knowledge of Him to some individuals, and does not make that knowledge available to others. But the Scripture does not actually *say* this. What Jesus does say in John 12:32 is, "And I, if I be lifted up from the earth, will *draw all men* to Myself." Now the Calvinist may immediately protest with, "If Jesus draws all men to Himself, all men will be saved." Well, if "draw all men" means "save all men," then all men will be saved, because that's what Jesus said. But we know all men are not saved, therefore, we must not interpret the word "draw" to mean "force to be saved through irresistible grace" (also, the word "draw" in both of these passages is indeed the same Greek word). So, we must ask, what does "draw all men" mean? Having been "lifted up" (crucified), what kind of "drawing" does Jesus do with "all men"? This is the work of the Holy Spirit, who comes to convict of sin, righteousness, and judgment (John 16:8). The Holy Spirit draws (woos, invites, warns, calls, illuminates, convicts, etc.) each man to the Person of Jesus Christ. This confirms that John 6:44 does *not* imply that God only draws some, for John 12:32 states that He draws *all*. These passages refer to the fact that God had to reconcile us to Himself through revealing Christ, because there is no way you or I can make our own way to God. He must initiate ("draw" and grant access) the relationship (this being the appropriate understanding of John 6:44). And again, Jesus is the "true light which, coming into the world, enlightens every man" (John 1:9). So even though God is always the one who initiates the relationship, He does offer that *drawing* to "every man." We then have the option to respond in faith that we might actually have the relationship.

The point again is what we see continually in Scripture. If you want to know God, you must know Him through a personal relationship with Jesus Christ who must reveal Himself to you personally. You can't know Him through the Law, through works, through Christian mechanics, or through being born into a Christian family, but you must respond to the Holy Spirit when he personally speaks to you and convicts you. Man's attempts to get to God through works, wisdom, persistence, etc. will never be successful. The only way for us to know God and have eternal life is through God's mercy and grace as He initiates (*draws* and grants access) a personal relationship with Jesus Christ.

So, today, if you hear His voice, do not harden your heart, as some do!

To my Calvinist friends, let me encourage you to find great joy in freely committing your life in faith and obedience to Christ. Jesus died for you, too. You do not have to continue living with the hope that you happen to be one of those He predestined. You, too, can respond personally (of your own volition) to the gospel. Now, for those who think that I am saying that all Calvinists are lost, that's not true. I simply want to make certain that each person's faith is indeed in Christ, and in Him alone! Calvinists believe (in general) that man is not able of his own volition to respond to God in personal faith, without God first instilling (forcing) "faith" within him. It is possible that some are living with the *hope* that their *desire* to know God is evidence of His predestining them. These, therefore, may conclude that they are saved (that they are one of the elect or the chosen), when, in fact, they have not personally trusted in Jesus.

The Elect

Paul said, "For this reason I endure all things for the sake of those who are *chosen*, that they also may obtain the salvation which is in Christ Jesus and with it eternal glory" (2 Timothy 2:10). You will notice that the King James Version says, "I endure all things for the *elect's* sakes." The words *chosen* and *elect* both come from the same Greek word.

Now, did you notice what Paul said here?

These "elect" are the Jews who were "chosen" to know God and share Him with the world. They were chosen, not to go to heaven over against others who would go to hell, but they were *chosen* that they might be a blessing to "all the families of the earth" (Genesis 12:3). But in their rebellion, many missed the salvation of their own Messiah! These are the very ones about whom Paul is so concerned in Romans 9:1–5.

Paul, in his letter here to Timothy, mentions his "enduring" suffering so that the *elect* "may" obtain salvation. These *chosen* Jews were lost, because they were seeking salvation through the works of the Law! True salvation is found only "in Christ Jesus," whom they rejected. Paul's effort is to convince them not to "deny" Christ (2 Timothy 2:12), but to obtain "eternal glory," a glory that they (the "chosen") will not "obtain" if they remain "faithless" (v. 13).

Please note that the *sons of Israel* in the Old Testament almost exclusively refers to descendants of the blood-line of Abraham (Jacob). The New Testament presents the spiritual application of the term "Israel" as true Christian believers (see Romans 4:9–16 and Galatians 3:6–9). The same is true with the concept and use of the term *chosen* (or *elect*). In the Old Testament we find God's people being the Israelites, who were chosen to be a channel by which God would reveal Himself to the world (Deuteronomy 7:6; 14:2). In the New Testament, we find both the historical and the spiritual application of this term. We've already noted the historical application from 2 Timothy 2:10, which actually speaks of the elect as *lost*. When given its spiritual connotation, the term *chosen* (*elect*) refers to the true children of God (those who exercise faith, or, as noted earlier in this book, as those who respond positively to His invitation – Matthew 22:14).

Therefore, the expression "the elect" or "the chosen" is terminology derived from its physical earthly connotation in the Old Testament, taking on a spiritual use in the New Testament. When we lift it straight out of the New Testament and begin defining the term outside of the context of the Old Testament, we end up with something foreign to its scriptural connotation. The Scriptures never say that God, from the beginning of time, elected certain people for salvation while deliberately excluding all others! God's Word never defines "the elect" in such fashion.

You Can Trust Him! Trust Him today!

"Therefore, let us fear lest, while a promise remains of entering His rest, any one of you should seem to have come short of it" (Hebrews 4:1). If God is the one who predestines a person's "coming short" of "entering His rest," then the truth is there is no promise for that person. Yet the Bible declares here that "a promise remains," and the encouragement to accept that promise is to every person (notice the singling out of "any one"). The only way you cannot "profit" from this promise is if you do not accept it with your own personal "faith" (Hebrews 4:2). The only way you will miss out on the eternal "rest" of heaven is if you are "disobedient" as were the Israelites (Hebrews 4:11).

So, while a promise remains, while the gospel is still available, seek the Lord while He may be found! Trust in Jesus, repent of your sin, and commit your life to Him! For God loves you, yes, *you*, whoever you are!

Scripture References by Chapter

Chapter 1

1 John 4:8, 16

Romans 6:23

1 John 4:10

Jonah 4:2, 11

Exodus 34:6–7

Joshua 24:15

Matthew 5:44–45

Matthew 9:36

Romans 5:6–10

Proverbs 1:29

Luke 6:27–38

Chapter 2

John 3:16

1 John 2:2

John 1:9

Romans 2:4–11

Acts 10:34-35

Romans 15:9–12

Acts 11:18

Matthew 22:10

Matthew 21:12–17

Numbers 21:8

John 7:37

Romans 1:16

Romans 3:9

Romans 10:11–13

Ephesians 3:6

Matthew 21:31–32

Matthew 5:45

Acts 16:30–31

John 3:15–17

Matthew 16:24–25

1 Peter 1:17

Romans 3:21–22

Genesis 12:3

Luke 2:10

Matthew 9:12–13

Isaiah 56:6–8

Chapter 3

Matthew 11:28–29   Matthew 9:9–13   Matthew 19:16–26
Matthew 22:1–14   Luke 14:23   Matthew 7:13
Luke 9:23   Matthew 4:17   Acts 17:30–31
Isaiah 45:22   Jeremiah 29:19; 35:15   Matthew 3:2
John 1:9   Romans 1:18–21   Psalm 34:8

Chapter 4

Matthew 23:37   Jeremiah 4:18–22   Jeremiah 8:18–22
Jeremiah 9:13   Numbers 14:11   Psalm 81:13–14
1 Timothy 2:3–4   Romans 11:32   Matthew 18:14
Luke 19:10   2 Corinthians 4:4   1 Corinthians 6:13
Ezekiel 33:11   Ezekiel 33:17, 20, 30–33   Ezekiel 18:28

2 Peter 3:9

Chapter 5

1 Timothy 2:5–6   1 John 3:16   2 Corinthians 9:7
Romans 2:4   Romans 12:1   John 3:18
Luke 10:29–37   Romans 3:9, 19, 25–26   John 12:46–47
Colossians 1:13   2 Corinthians 5:15   Hebrews 2:9
1 John 4:9   Romans 5:6–10   Luke 23:34
1 Corinthians 2:2   1 Timothy 1:15

Chapter 6

Matthew 28:19–20   Acts 1:8   John 1:7
Matthew 22:9–10   2 Corinthians 5:10–11   Romans 1:5
1 John 1:5   Titus 1:2   Romans 9:1–3
Romans 10:1   Romans 11:14   Romans 10:13
2 Corinthians 5:18–21   Romans 1:16   John 5:18, 34
Luke 5:32   1 Corinthians 9:22   John 20:31

Chapter 7

Deuteronomy 30:19–20

Romans 5:1–2

Romans 4:12, 16

Romans 3:26, 28

John 1:12

Acts 11:17

Acts 26:17–18

Acts 2:37–38

1 Peter 1:9

Acts 17:26–27

Isaiah 55:6

Jeremiah 29:13

Job 1:9–11

2 Corinthians 9:6–7

Hosea 6:6

Psalm 32:8–9

Romans 11:15–23

Jeremiah 36:3

Romans 3:22–28

Romans 10:17–21

Matthew 19:16–21

John 5:34, 40

Proverbs 1:24–29

Jeremiah 18:5–11

Matthew 5:30

Luke 13:3

Hebrews 12:14

Luke 14:16–20

Luke 7:30

Matthew 5:20

Matthew 21:28–32

Isaiah 30:15

Jeremiah 5:22, 25

Chapter 8

Matthew 22:1–14

2 Corinthians 5:21

Luke 19:11–27

Isaiah 66:4

2 Corinthians 5:10

Romans 1:20–26

Luke 3:8–9

Romans 2:4–8

Isaiah 5

Jeremiah 22:8–9

Matthew 7:13–14, 21–27

Luke 11:13

James 1:5–7

John 4:10

Revelation 3:5

Romans 11:20

Hebrews 3:19

Psalm 69:18, 28

Isaiah 1:18–20

Jeremiah 4:18; 2:17; 6:19

Ezekiel 18:1–32

John 16

Hebrews 3:12–19

Hebrews 10:26–39

2 Corinthians 6:1

Acts 7:51–52

Isaiah 55:6–7

1 Thessalonians 5:2

Mark 8:35–36

Chapter 9

1 John 4:16

Galatians 4:17

Romans 11:32

Jude 5

Leviticus 19:18

Matthew 22:39

Luke 6:35   Deuteronomy 10:19   Psalm 145:17

Chapter 10

2 Timothy 3:15   Proverbs 30:5   Titus 1:2
Jeremiah 29:11–13   Luke 19:10   Matthew 7:7–8
2 Chronicles 15:2   Acts 2:38   Romans 10:9–13

Conclusion

2 Peter 1:20–21   2 Timothy 3:16   Proverbs 30:5
Titus 1:2   Romans 8:29–30   Ephesians 1:1–12
Romans 8:15   2 Thessalonians 1:8; Acts 13:38–49
                     2:10–14

John 15:16   Luke 14:26   1 John 3:15
Romans 9:1–16   Galatians 3:7   Romans 11:32
Malachi 1:1–5   Jeremiah 18:5–11   Hebrews 12:15–17
Romans 9:17–18   Exodus 9:13–17, 29   Romans 9:21
2 Timothy 2:21   Romans 11:22–23   Romans 9:19–23
Romans 9:1–3   Romans 10:3, 9–13   Romans 11:11–23
Romans 11:28–32   Hebrews 3:7–8, 15–19 2 Corinthians 6:2
John 6:44   Romans 9:31–32   John 12:32
John 16:8   John 1:9   2 Timothy 2:10–13
Genesis 12:3   Romans 4:9–16   Galatians 3:6–9
Deuteronomy 7:6; 14:2 Matthew 22:14   Hebrews 4:1–2, 11

Self–Study Worksheet

INSTRUCTIONS: Read each selected passage. Write out your answers to the simple questions using the truths found in each text.

Chapter 1: God is love!

1. <u>Matthew 5:44–45</u> To share in the character and nature of God (to be like Him and do what He does), what are we to do?

2. <u>Luke 6:35–36</u> Is God kind just to *some* ungrateful and evil men? Why are we to be merciful to our enemies?

3. <u>Matthew 9:36</u> Did Jesus have compassion for just *some* of the multitude, or for all?

Chapter 2: God shares His love with all people!

1. <u>Numbers 21:8</u> (John 3:14–15) Who could have looked at the bronze serpent and have been healed?

2. <u>John 3:16</u> Whom did God love so much that He sent His only Son, Jesus, to die?

3. <u>1 John 2:2</u> Jesus is the propitiation for whose sins other than ours?

4. <u>John 7:37</u> Whom did Jesus exclude in this call?

5. <u>Matthew 16:24–27</u> Can a man predestined to heaven "forfeit" his soul? To whom was this call given?

6. <u>Acts 10:34–35 & Romans 2:11; 3:21–22</u> These verses are about salvation. Is God impartial with each man?

7. <u>Romans 10:11–13</u> Is there "no distinction" such that "whosoever" may call upon the Lord?

Chapter 3: God invites each person to Himself!

1. <u>Matthew 11:28–29</u> To whom does Jesus extend this invitation?

2. <u>Matthew 22:1–14</u> The parable is an all-inclusive invitation requiring a response of the *will* and *submission* (wedding-clothes). Who are the few who are "chosen"?

3. <u>Matthew 7:13–14</u> To whom did Jesus extend this call to enter the path that leads to life?

4. <u>Acts 17:30</u> To whom does God declare this call to repent?

5. <u>Isaiah 45:22</u> Whom does God invite to be saved by turning (repenting)?

6. <u>John 1:9</u> What does Jesus do for every person?

Chapter 4: God desires all men to be saved!

1. <u>Matthew 23:37</u> Did Jesus really "desire" to save Jerusalem? Why didn't He?

2. <u>Jeremiah 4:18–22; 8:18–22</u> Why was God so broken-hearted? Why weren't His people "restored"?

3. <u>1 Timothy 2:3–4</u> Does God really "desire" all men to saved?

4. <u>Matthew 18:14</u> Is it God's will for any person to perish?

5. <u>Ezekiel 33:11</u> What is God's will for people who are wicked?

6. <u>2 Peter 3:9</u> What is God's "wish" for all people?

Chapter 5: Jesus died for every single person who has ever lived!

1. <u>1 Timothy 2:5–6</u> What did Jesus do for all people?

2. <u>2 Corinthians 5:15</u> For whom did Jesus die?

3. <u>Hebrews 2:9</u> For whom did Jesus "taste death"?

4. <u>Luke 23:34</u> On the cross, for whom was Jesus praying?

5. <u>1 Timothy 1:15</u> Whom did Jesus come to save? Are you a sinner?

Chapter 6: Jesus sends His disciples to every person in the world!

1. <u>Matthew 28:19–20</u> Which nations are we to evangelize?

2. <u>Matthew 22:9–10</u> When we go witnessing, whom will we invite on God's behalf?

3. Romans 9:1–3 Did Paul love these lost men more than God did?

4. 2 Corinthians 5:18–21 Is the "begging" that God does through us an authentic plea to all men?

5. John 5:34 Did Jesus want these lost men to hear and be saved?

Chapter 7: God gives every man the choice to trust Him or reject Him!

1. Deuteronomy 30:19–20 Can any person choose life?

2. Acts 11:17 When does the Holy Spirit enter a person's life?

3. 1 Peter 1:9 Does "faith" come before or after salvation?

4. Romans 11:20–23 Why are some branches (people) "broken off"? Can they be grafted back in?

5. Jeremiah 36:3 What was God hoping every man would do so that He would forgive?

6. Proverbs 1:24–29 Can a person choose to fear the Lord?

7. Jeremiah 18:5–11 What is God's criterion for what He does in His sovereignty?

8. Luke 7:30 What was God's purpose for the Pharisees?

9. Isaiah 30:15 Why are some not saved?

Chapter 8: There are severe consequences to rejecting God's call!

1. Matthew 22:7, 13 Why did these suffer such consequences?

2. Isaiah 66:4 Why were these men judged so harshly? (see also: Jeremiah 22:8–9)

3. <u>Hebrews 10:29</u> Can the Spirit of grace be insulted?

4. <u>2 Corinthians 6:1</u> Can God's grace be received in vain?

5. <u>Acts 7:51</u> Can the Holy Spirit be resisted?

Chapter 9: Some people believe that God may not really love you!

1. <u>Romans 11:32</u> To whom has God purposed to show His mercy?

2. <u>Jude 5</u> Who does God ultimately destroy? (see also: Hebrews 3:19)

3. <u>Luke 6:35</u> Who am I to love? Does God love them, too?

Chapter 10: God's Word is pure! Trust Him! He loves you! He's told you!

1. <u>2 Timothy 3:15</u> Can one find truth that leads to salvation in God's Word?

2. <u>Luke 19:10</u> Whom did Jesus come to save? Are you lost?

3. <u>1 John 3:16</u> How do we know God loves us?